Contents

National Health

JOHN VAIZEY

Martin Robertson

First published in 1984 by Martin Robertson & Company Ltd.,
108 Cowley Road, Oxford OX4 1JF.

British Library Cataloguing in Publication Data

Vaizey, John
  Health
  1. Great Britain—National Health Service—History
  I. Title
  321'.0941   RA395.G6

  ISBN 0–85520–695–0
  ISBN 0–85520–696–9 Pbk

Typeset by Katerprint Co Ltd, Oxford.
Printed and bound in Great Britain by
Billing and Sons Ltd, Worcester.

Preface and Acknowledgements

Cut, cut, cut – these have been the headlines about the health service while this book was being written. I have deliberately tried to stand back from this essentially sterile controversy about which political party will spend more on the NHS, to try to focus the discussion on what seems to me to be more long-term issues.

Health care has been fundamentally altered by modern drugs and other developments, though many people are (rightly) suspicious of over-medication, and feel that modern medicine has taken a fundamentally wrong turn by becoming so technologically based. I do not share this view. I do hold strongly, however, to the opinion that prevention is better than cure, and that it is this side of medicine that needs to be developed. Immunization and vaccination have wrought miracles. Pure water and clean air have been no less miraculous.

My fundamental thesis is that the incidence of illness is changing, and that modern developments require far more emphasis on home-based care. Many hospitals *ought* to be and *will* be closed. That is not to say that the hospital has no future. Far from it. But the hospital is not a first port of call – it is a specialized facility that is there for cases that cannot be treated elsewhere.

I do not think modern medicine can be cheap. Though the proportion of the British national income spent on health care is lower than elsewhere, this is to make a virtue out of necessity. More will have to be spent. But it will not be spent, whichever party is in power, if all the money has to come from taxation. The issue is how to harness the citizen's own purchasing power. Nobody thinks scarce medical resources should go only to those who can pay. But we can all pay for some preventive medicine, and some routine medical care. I hope readers will not assume that this is not an arguable case. It is carefully argued here, so as to try to defuse the debate.

The book was written before the Griffiths Report on management was published. But the argument that I have produced is essentially on similar lines.

It will be obvious that many of my ideas and facts are drawn from Office of Health Economics work, which I gratefully acknowledge. *The OHE has no responsibility at all for the way I have used this work.*

I am especially grateful to Professor George Teeling-Smith, OBE; David Taylor; Tom Vaizey, who did a lot of the leg work; Diana Wood who was the secretary who worked hard on it; and above all my editor, Venetia Pollock.

John Vaizey
Windsor
December 1983

Introduction

The way in which we organize health care and pay for it cannot be decided in the abstract, philosophically: it must be the result of a sequence of answers to a series of questions, all interconnected but changing in their nature as reality itself changes. The incidence of illness is not static: some diseases become less virulent, while new ones appear. Above all, the understanding of medicine deepens and broadens all the time; treatment changes, and so what might have been a desirable health-care system in 1948 has become unsuitable for 1988 because the problems have changed. Accordingly, the emphasis of this book is on change – the changes in medicine itself, both those that have taken place and those that may be reasonably foreseen, and the changes in the economy and in society which have already affected health and are likely to do so in the future.

In chapter 1, I try to define what is meant by modern health care. Chapter 2 discusses two major trends that have become evident over the past century. First, rising living standards have themselves very considerably reduced death (mortality) and illness (morbidity): people have become better nourished, better clothed, better housed, more hygienic, more conscious of health. Second, a medical revolution, beginning with antiseptics then moving on to antibiotics, has greatly reduced infectious diseases which are not based on viruses. Smallpox has been eliminated throughout the world, and tuberculosis is now rare in Britain and other advanced countries. Thus an improvement in the environment and several major advances in medicine have very considerably reduced death rates, especially among children and young people, and in certain major respects they have reduced morbidity.

Chapter 3, on the developing countries, shows that what for us are essentially historical events are for them daily reality. Consequently, the pattern of health care in the Third World bears a marked resemblance to what used to be the case in the highly industrialized countries. But, of course, since they are repeating recognized experiences, they can be helped more quickly. Hence the drop in death rates in Third World countries and the consequent population explosion will be far greater than could at one time have been imagined.

The discussion then turns to the problems facing Britain today. Most illnesses are no longer severe and can be dealt with mainly by general practitioners, local chemists and other primary health-care workers. But some illnesses are sufficiently serious to need the hospital service. This service has a declining number of customers – in the sense that the number of nights spent in hospital is down – but those customers it does have tend to suffer from singularly recalcitrant diseases, such as cancer, heart disease and mental illness, and those of an incurable nature, like multiple sclerosis.

Looking ahead, then, we can foresee a considerable increase in expenditure on these major killers, which will be very costly to treat because the initial stages of a 'breakthrough' will involve a great many trial-and-error attempts and much further research into the fundamental life sciences and into pharmaceutical developments. But success in overcoming these killer diseases in our lifetime appears to be a distinct possibility. Such advances in medicine will not only save life and diminish morbidity but will also improve the quality of life for many. It is difficult to assign an economic value to this development, but it will mean a dramatic improvement in the nation's health.

Until now a health-care system has meant exactly the opposite – an illness-care system. But people are beginning to think that the word 'health' ought to mean what it says. In this book I hope to show that modern health care has many facets, that it covers both positive preventive medicine and those personal, social, psychological, mental, physical and medical problems which people take to their doctors because they feel such problems have become too much for them to bear. I hope to show too that advances in modern medicine have changed people's expectations and demands, which in turn have affected the way in which they use their general practitioners. The increasingly technological nature of modern medicine has also affected what the doctor can do and how he or she makes use of hospital services. Hospitals in their turn have also been affected. The problems and costs of all these facets of modern health care, their effects and the changes that are occurring in all these fields are discussed in greater detail in chapters 5 to 9.

The effects of recent changes in modern health care are to be seen in differing degrees in all high-income, industrial and post-industrial societies. Though the discussion will centre on the United Kingdom, the arguments apply equally to all other OECD countries and, to a lesser extent, also to the Soviet Union and its occupied European territories. Chapter 10 reviews briefly the different systems of health care in Europe and raises questions concerning alternative methods of provision in Britain and of funding, which are pursued in chapter 11, where the discussion turns to the future of health care in the United Kingdom.

Medical care must be seen always in the context of changing patterns of living; the diseases that medicine tackles are the products of the age. Yet there is a perennial tendency for health-care systems to be set up to deal predominantly with yesterday's rather than tomorrow's problems. The thesis of this book, that health and illness are consequences of the way in which we live and that medicine makes a marginal (but often crucial) difference to our survival, though certainly a difference to our comfort, puts medical care and its relation to illness and death into what I believe to be a radically new perspective.

1

Positive Health Care

No absolute definition of health care means much, since it implies a human being ticking over like a machine without a soul, with no capacity for misery. But it is possible to claim that any given change is a move in the direction of, or away from, 'health' as commonly understood. In a modern health service, whether publicly or privately provided, a great deal of effort is devoted to the concept of positive health.

The World Health Organization is one of the more effective of the United Nations' specialized agencies. It has adopted, however, a singularly unhelpful definition of health: 'Health is a state of complete physical, mental and social wellbeing, and not merely the absence of disease or infirmity.' This definition is unhelpful because few people can be found to fulfil such stringent terms. Yet it is significant because it illustrates a modern phenomenon: whatever the crisis or problem that afflicts the human body or spirit, from cancer to grief, from rheumatism to unacceptable housing, the cry is to send for the doctor. A rise in the number of broken marriages, for example, is now increasing the level of demand for medical care, broadly considered, since the doctor and his or her team of community nurses and other paramedical professionals will be concerned with such matters as the vulnerability of children of broken homes, the psychic health of the patients whose marriages have collapsed and the problems of income and housing for those in need. In short, today the doctor is the focal point of a very wide range of concerns. He or she has taken on the part of the parson, the social worker, the older brother; and as, increasingly, we turn to the doctor in moments of childish despair, so the doctor becomes more and more a parental figure, attracting our love and our hate but assuming in our unconscious minds a role of perennial omnipotence.

1

Only psychoanalysts assume this role consciously. Other doctors merely accept it as part of their profession's new broad-spectrum image. Many reject it utterly and have become consciously scientific instead, relying predominantly upon tests and analyses of physically measurable phenomena. These two tendencies, doctor as priest and doctor as scientist, have played a major part in creating the pattern of medicine as it now exists, and together they determine to some degree what will happen in medical care.

Since it is difficult to define health satisfactorily, perhaps it would be better to start by describing ill-health. From time to time everyone feels under the weather, bothered by aches and pains, depressed or out of sorts, but mostly such symptoms are recognized as passing problems and are quickly dismissed. However, eventually there comes a time when the problems become so insistent, so unpleasant, painful or alarming, that they affect the quality of life of the person concerned, and so he or she feels the need for help. The condition may be an illness in the strictly old-fashioned sense of that word – that is, caused by an infection, a virus or an accident. It may be that the person has eaten, drunk or smoked too much. It may be the onset of a recognizable disease such as multiple sclerosis, for which there is as yet no known cure. It may be an allergy to modern manufactured products or a painful infirmity brought on by old age. Whatever it is, the fact that it has brought the patient to the doctor defines it as ill-health.

Sometimes interpersonal problems, a feeling of inadequacy in a person's chosen employment or in his or her social circle or the self-imposition of unrealistic ambitions sets up stresses which create the psychosomatic aches and pains that prompts a person to visit the doctor. But as determinants of ill-health such social and psychological problems are just as important as genuine physical factors, for both make people seek medical aid. As Dr Jonathan Miller points out in his book *The Body in Question*:

Falling ill is not something that happens to us, it is a choice we make as a result of things happening to us. It is an action we take when we feel unacceptably odd. Obviously there are times when this choice is taken out of the victim's hands: he may be so

2

overwhelmed by events that he plans no active part in what happens next and is brought to the doctor by friends or relatives, stricken or helpless. But that is rare. Most people who fall ill have chosen to cast themselves in the role of patient. Viewing their unfortunate situation, they see themselves as sick people and begin to act differently. *

In 1962 the Office of Health Economics was set up by the pharmaceutical industry, and financed by it, to undertake research into the economic aspects of medical care. It is run by Professor George Teeling-Smith, an academic of distinction, and its governing body is autonomous. Its reports have gained wide acceptance for their authority and their lucidity. This body sets out the problem clearly:

In very broad terms ill-health is defined as circumstances in which the patient experiences physical, mental or even social symptoms and in which these are accepted as medically significant by the doctor. . . . therefore ill-health could be defined as what the doctor decides: it is created, or accepted, in a medical consultation. Thereafter the medical machinery starts up and, whatever the problem, a medical solution is looked for.

The problem thus may not be medical in the strictest sense of the word, but once a doctor is called in, it becomes a medical one and is treated in a medical fashion. With the scientific basis of medicine so much to the fore, the diagnosis and treatment of the problem becomes scientific. Today this also makes it respectable.

It is respectable and socially acceptable to be ill, whereas it is often unacceptable just to 'cop out' or to be labelled a failure, wicked or irresponsible. Once an inadequacy has been taken to the doctor and diagnosed as a medical problem, it too becomes a matter of ill-health. The doctor's ability to call us 'ill' is a face-saver: no longer do we have to say that our social life is in ruins, that our job has gone or that we row endlessly with our spouse. The labelling of inadequacy, joblessness

* Jonathan Miller, *The Body in Question*, London, Jonathan Cape, 1978, p. 49.

and marital discord as medically confirmed illnesses enables us to seek help without shame, and the fact that this is so is the product of a much deeper psychological and social understanding of the problems under-lying ill-health. Gradually over the years language has altered to remain in touch with such changes in attitude; now an illegitimate child and its parent can be called a 'one-parent family'; a stand-up fistfight may be described as a 'difficult interpersonal relationship'. In the same way 'ill-health' has come to describe a multitude of sins: illness is what the doctor treats.

However, it must be made clear that ill-health is not the unavoidable and wholly excusable consequence of exposure to external challenges. It is the failure of the body or mind to adapt to such changes.

Today a patient who says he is ill – and increasingly his doctor is likely to say, 'OK, you *are* ill' – is plugged into the medical-care system, and the process becomes self-confirming. Both the public and the medical profession seem to accept ill-health as unavoidable and as the responsibility of the health service rather than the individual. As a result there is continual expansion of the demand for health services. People are expecting more and more from their doctors and are taking an increasing number of problems to them, looking to them for counsel, comfort and care as well as cure.

That they are doing this is not surprising, for deeper scientific understanding has enabled doctors to accomplish more and more. Although there is a limit to what medicine can beneficially achieve, the spectrum that it covers is expanding in leaps and bounds; as a result, so are people's expectations. Today anxiety can be relieved with a pill: there is no need to contact a priest. Feeling vaguely unwell can often be traced to some chemical imbalance: there is no need to sit and suffer. When we consider that until comparatively recently medical care all too often meant nursing the sick by making them comfortable and relieving their pain whenever possible, the advances that have been made are most impressive. Until the 1930s doctors had few drugs to offer. They set broken bones, sawed off limbs, stitched up gaping wounds, succoured the dying and brought reassurance by their presence. Scientific and technological progress has changed the picture altogether.

Positive Health Care

As I have mentioned, modern medical care is an amalgam of two tendencies, the roles of doctor as priest and doctor as scientist, and in particular it is the latter who has enabled many of the major breakthroughs in medicine to be made, for he or she has been concerned primarily with the accuracy of diagnosis and the effectiveness of treatment in terms of statistics. This scientific approach to illness, which has also been applied to the use of vaccines for immunization and to pharmaceutical-based treatments, has led to the abandonment of a large number of treatments when tests have revealed their inefficacy and, equally, to the successful use of new drugs when they have proved their worth. Scientifically minded doctors have joined in highly sophisticated experiments which include double-blind trials: for example, tests in which drugs and placebos are used and those who administer the tests have no idea which patient is receiving a drug and which a placebo. They have also helped with the evaluation of such tests over hundreds of thousands of observations until cause and effect have been scientifically and statistically established. As a result, medicine today depends a great deal on statistical techniques to provide information about the probability of outcomes as related to the causal agent.

However, since medicine is concerned with the individual human being, there is an uncomfortable disparity between what is scientifically true – that is, what leads to a high probability that something will happen – and what is individually true. What is generally true may well not be at all true for individual cases. It is highly likely that most people will die in their early seventies; some, however, will live to be over 100, and others will die in their forties. Most people will benefit from a drug properly prescribed for their correctly diagnosed illness, but a minority will not benefit or will be actively harmed. These latter are the cases that make the headlines: Thalidomide was originally a successful tranquillizer with few side-effects for most people until it was found that, if taken by pregnant mothers, it caused their fetuses to become malformed. The adverse propaganda that Thalidomide and similar drugs receive may be justified, but it is based largely upon the most fundamental misapprehension of the nature of risk in all human activities: 100 per cent successful outcomes can never be guaranteed,

5

only a high probability of success. An exactly parallel instance has to do with cigarette smoking. Everybody knows somebody who is as fit as can be, has lived to a ripe old age and smokes forty cigarettes a day. The graveyards are full of the hundreds of thousands of those of whom that has not been true: they smoked themselves to death. Similarly, people not wearing seat belts occasionally crawl unharmed from a blazing car in which they would have been trapped had they been strapped in. Thousands of others have been killed or seriously maimed because they were not wearing seat belts when accidents occurred.

The fundamental question to be asked of all therapeutic procedures, therefore, is how far the balance of beneficial outcomes predominates over harmful ones. It is essential to assess the probability of a given outcome – in particular, to assess the risk of failure. Some procedures are entirely riskless (such as giving up smoking) and have consequences that are entirely beneficial; other activities are so risky that they ought rarely to be undertaken – at the moment heart transplants are an example. The frontiers of riskiness alter as some procedures become safer and some suddenly develop new side-effects. As the public becomes more aware of risk, it seeks to avoid what it regards as unsafe procedures; it becomes what the City would call 'more aware of down-side potential'. This awareness shifts the borders of acceptable risk-taking, so that hitherto common procedures, like taking an aspirin for a headache, are ruled out of court because it is now known that in some instances aspirin causes internal bleeding. Thus the activities of the health-care professions are to be seen in terms of probabilities. Health care is about making it more likely that people will be healthy.

But in certain matters people are completely illogical. A death rate of 1 in 1 million for a drug would cause it to be withdrawn from use. There are surgical procedures in which a death rate of 1 in 100 is common and acceptable. But cigarette smoking is actually much more risky than our hypothetical drug, so if it were a pharmaceutical, tobacco would undoubtedly be banned, as (probably) would alcohol. Why is it that the drug is perceived as being more risky than the operation, and both are perceived as more risky than cigarettes and drink?

When trying to weigh the benefit of any treatment against its outcome, not only the risk of failure but also the economic and financial costs must be taken into account: what was once known fashionably in economic circles as a cost–benefit analysis must be carried out. In general an activity such as a heart transplant will be undertaken only when all the benefits, in the widest possible sense of the word, outweigh all the costs. Sometimes the benefits may be spread over such a long period that they have to be discounted; at other times they may be direct (the saving of the patient's life) or indirect (benefiting his employer and saving long-term social security payments). Similarly, the costs will also be both direct (say, the operation itself) and indirect (those that are carried by organizations other than the hospital, such as research). From this series of calculations it can be determined whether the yield of a procedure is greater than its cost: procedures can then be ranked by their yields as well as by their riskiness.

Thus there are two sets of calculations to be taken into account when assessing whether or not to carry out a given operation or medical treatment: the riskiness of a procedure, as measured by the likelihood of beneficial outcomes, and the cost–benefit, as measured by whether the yield is greater than the cost. Many of these calculations are never undertaken in full. In this matter medical care is by no means alone. Much education, for example, would never be undertaken if it were to be judged coldly on its results, measured in this fashion. But it is often because such an analysis is not carried through that health service policy-makers find themselves in a parlous position.

No one could define, even broadly, the most cost-effective health-care system, so people are led by fashion to demand ineffective care or by panic to demand absolute safety – which is unattainable. Ideally, one would like to rank medical-care procedures in order, so that the cheapest, which yield most benefit, are widely available and the most expensive, which yield least benefit, are less generally available. But the public, seeing medical care as 'life-saving', will subscribe thousands of pounds to pay for a child (described in the newspapers as a 'kiddy') to go to America for some dubious and expensive treatment for a rare condition, while it will not support widespread anti-smoking campaigns, whose success would save thousands of lives; equally, people will work flat-out to raise money for a scanner for their local hospital when it would be more cost-effective, and would help more people, if the money were spent on more hip-replacement operations, which are now cheap and safe and restore mobility to many elderly people.

However, it is not surprising that the public is bewildered by the wide variety of medical treatments that are available and finds it difficult to choose between their relative merits and their cost-effectiveness, for there has been a continuous revolution in medicine, especially in pharmacological innovations, since the 1930s. This wave of innovations appeared to be at an end in the 1960s, but that proved not to be the case; and now even more major developments are expected which will enable many diseases to be treated that hitherto have not been susceptible to medical intervention. This prospect has raised the expectations of patients, and they are absolutely right to expect more, since the basis of their expectations is in fact a realistic view of what the medical profession and the drug industry will have to offer in the future. At the same time, the boundaries of illness are also expanding. When a patient comes to a doctor with a problem, there are now whole teams of specialist workers who may be called upon to help — nurses, radio-therapists, radiologists, pharmacists, physio-therapists, paramedics and others — all of whom are encouraged to alleviate suffering.

Several aspects of this expectation of improvement in an ever-increasing range of health care require discussion. First, in a genuine sense, it is immediately cost-raising. It is true that, to take an extreme case, a major organ transplant can now (and will even more in the future) not only save life and alleviate suffering but also return the patient to productive work. Its economic benefits therefore sometimes outweigh its cost. But the immediate effect of the procedure is to raise costs, no matter by whom they are borne — the patient, his employer, or the taxpayer. This is not true of all medical procedures — for example, a simple, cheap vaccine has eliminated most forms of tuberculosis — but in general more medical care, especially more effective medical care, means more expenditure.

The second consequence of medical advance is a shift in the pattern of medical care. The general practitioner or, as the jargon has it, the primary medical-care team, takes an increasingly active role in dealing with an ever-growing range of conditions; partly, for reasons already given, because it makes the embarrassing social and personal difficulty socially acceptable, and also because it can actually *do* more. At the same time more people are likely to visit a hospital at least once in their lives, if only for an X-ray or a body scan. Most will be out-patients; those few who do become resident will stay only briefly. The hotel element of hospital life will decrease, but the use of the hospital for diagnostic investigations, sophisticated technical treatment and acute cases will increase. The position of those using hospitals because they are chronic long-stay patients – the mentally handicapped, geriatric and severely physically disabled, who are to a considerable degree social rather than medical patients – will also change with advancements in medicine. The upshot of this series of shifts in treatment will be to raise the cost of the different parts of the medical-care system dealing with those who suffer from ill-heath.

There is too the fundamental question of preventive medicine. It is increasingly being shown that good health depends upon good habits: on exercise, a moderate, well balanced diet, a sensible alcohol intake, the avoidance of drug abuse, no smoking. Careful driving also prevents accidents, which often lead to expensive medical problems, so wearing seat belts and observing the speed limits can also be forms of preventive medicine, as can adequately heated and ventilated houses. These examples may not seem to be related to health care in the conventional sense of the word, but they are all very important indeed in preventing illness and therefore in promoting positive health care.

2

The Historical Background

Both the reasons why people die and the age of death have changed radically over the last 200 years in the Western world. British data show the facts clearly and could be repeated for every other advanced country. Until the eighteenth century the population of Britain grew only very slowly, controlled by high birth and high mortality rates.

Although Jenner discovered vaccination at the end of the eighteenth century and although Guy's, St George's, the Westminster, the London and the Middlesex hospitals were all founded between 1720 and 1745, they did not initially have a marked effect on the death rate. The medical profession moved out of the Dark Ages very slowly indeed, and people took a long time to become aware of the nature of diseases, how they travelled and how their virulence could be prevented. Little was done to control the conditions under which people lived in the cities. Overcrowding, slum tenements and sewage drains which oozed into the fresh-water supply encouraged infectious diseases to rampage through the population; raging epidemics of cholera and typhoid were frequent – one such epidemic was so serious that Parliament passed the first Public Health Act, as a result, in 1848. It was estimated that between 1848 and 1872 thirty-six children under 5 years old died out of every thousand born. Among adults communicable diseases were still the main cause of death: in 1870 32 per cent of males died from infectious diseases such as cholera, typhoid, influenza and tuberculosis; measles and diphtheria were also prevalent and were particularly killers of children. Gradually, however, towards the end of the nineteenth century and during the earlier years of this century, cleaner water supplies, more nutritious foods, environmental improvements such as sewage works and preventive measures such as vaccination and immunization began to change the mortality rates for the better.

Figures for Britain show a doubling of the population every quarter-century from 1800 to 1875, when the rate of increase began to slow down. Initially, a higher birth rate (arising from earlier marriage) played its part, as it did in the doubling of the Irish population between 1800 and 1845, when the famine and its corollaries – emigration and illness – halved it. But the major cause of the population 'explosion', to use a modern cliché, was better nutrition and hygiene and better housing, running water and drainage systems. Public health care and medical techniques then became the main life-savers.

As the quality of medicine improved and the standard of living rose, the population increased because more children lived longer. Large families with ten or eleven children all living to maturity became commonplace in late Victorian and early Edwardian times. As people grew richer, they restricted the size of their families. The very poor needed children as an insurance and to provide earning power. The better-off married later and controlled their fertility, from 1870 onwards, by elementary contraceptive techniques. It is known that abortion was widespread – especially, for instance, in France. Charles Bradlaugh and Mrs Besant were prosecuted as far back as 1877 for publishing a pamphlet on methods of birth control.

The 1930s saw the big medical breakthrough, with the revolutionary pharmacological innovations, modern anaesthetics, sulphanilomides, X-rays and greatly improved surgical techniques. The discovery and development of penicillin and antibiotics in the 1940s and 1950s greatly reduced infections. Today the population of the United Kingdom has stabilized with a steady low rate of births and a low mortality rate. Life expectancy is now double the nineteenth-century average. But, of course, we will all die sooner or later. Among those who died in 1980, the following causes of death predominated:

290,000	'diseases of the circulatory system' (of which most were either heart disease or heart attack)
130,000	cancer
83,000	'diseases of the respiratory system' (mostly 'flu and pneumonia among the elderly)
70,000	strokes and similar diseases

20,000   accidents (nearly 6,000 in traffic accidents)
16,000   diseases of the digestive system

A few thousand also died from infectious disease, various other causes and from what could really be called old age. These were largely people born before or during the First World War. Most of the men were 70 or over, most of the women 80 or over.

It must be remembered that what people die of is not necessarily what they are ill with (see below, p. 16). There is a sharp distinction between mortality (death) and morbidity (illness), and this must always be clearly borne in mind. However, what these figures do show is that infection rarely kills: fewer than 1 per cent of deaths today are from infection, but over 50 per cent are caused by heart and respiratory diseases and cancer. The deaths of children under 5 in the United Kingdom constitute only about 3 per cent of the total deaths for any given year. Children rarely die now.

These major changes in the pattern of when and why people die are extremely interesting and can be considered in various ways. One could say that the crude death rate was halved between 1841 and 1981. It has not been a steady reduction following an even curve; the decline accelerated between 1881 and 1921 because home and working conditions improved so markedly. Most recently the drop in the proportion of children in the population as a whole has further increased the fall; it has made the *standardized* mortality rate decline by four. In other words, the risk of dying at any given age has fallen by four times today by comparison with the past.

Another way of looking at this question of death rates is to talk about life. A child born in 1841 was expected to live for thirty-five years: now a child is likely to live to well over 70, especially if a girl. Most of the improvement has been brought about by better child care: 6.6 per cent of children under 5 died in the 1840s, whereas the proportion is now 0.04 per cent. At the age of 15 in 1841 people could expect to live to over 60; now they can look forward to living to over 70. Life expectancy for men at the age of 45 has hardly varied at all over the past century and a half, though it has risen by ten years for women. Almost the same is true for people aged 65.

13

The reason for interpreting these figures in a variety of ways is to demonstrate that it is untrue to say that 'we' are living longer. What is true is that infants now rarely die, and they used to die like flies. Why, then, do people say that 'we' are living longer? Basically because the proportion of older people is rising and because the number of younger people is declining as a result of falling birth-rates. There are more elderly people around, which fosters the illusion that people are living longer. The decline in infant mortality occurred generally before modern medicine had really become established, but once it got into its stride it had a further effect on lowering the death rate, which fell for infants and young people between the years 1941 and 1961 (except during the war), whereas for those over 50 the death rate has scarcely fallen at all for many years. Perhaps the most dramatic way of making the same point is to say that in the early 1840s half the funerals were for people under 14 and only a fifth were for those over 65, whereas now only one coffin in fifty is ordered for a child, while three-quarters are for elderly people. The Victorians mourned their children; we mourn our parents.

There is discussion below of the problems of pregnancy, abortion and neo-natal mortality, but here it must suffice to say that death in childbirth is now rare. Today the problems are of quite a different order.

These new patterns of death have had a considerable effect on our society, on our medical services, on the needs of the ill and on the type of care they require. Death is not illness, but the longer death is postponed, the more likely people are to become ill. However, what they suffer from at different times in their life cycle and what they need to help them has changed considerably. This is the new pattern of illness. The ill now rarely die.

It is an inescapable fact that much more medical care is now expended on elderly people, as there are so many more of them, but their lives are not so much prolonged by this care as made, one hopes, more tolerable and more comfortable. As will be seen, much modern medicine also concentrates on the problems of the middle-aged, especially cancer and cardio-vascular diseases. Medical care does not prolong life: it makes it better.

For children the major medical victory has been the control of infections. The greater part of this battle was won in the nineteenth and early twentieth centuries through improved hygiene and nutrition. But since 1931 dramatic progress has been made by immunization. Death rates among children under 14 fell by five-sixths between 1931 and 1961. Most deaths were prevented by the elimination of tuberculosis and diphtheria and the virtual elimination of measles, whooping cough and scarlet fever, almost entirely the consequence of immunization. Preventive medicine scored a moderate but still remarkable triumph when child deaths halved between 1946 and 1961 – a drop in the bucket by comparison with what happened in Victorian times but still worthy of note.

Children still fall ill, but they are not usually severely physically ill. Actual illness has not diminished by much; the *severity* of illness has, however, diminished markedly. That is one of the reasons why children's hospitals are closing and why those that remain open are switching, for the most part, to caring for relatively rare conditions. Paediatrics is now the special study of the basically healthy child. Of course, too, the social problems of childhood have called forth an army of social workers to pick up the pieces of family breakdown – caused not only by divorce – and of psychiatric and emotional problems. There is also a growing band of handicapped children who now survive both pregnancy, despite high abortion rates, and their first year of life. These are the chronic handicapped, those with spina bifida, Down's syndrome and the spastics. They are not ill, but they need care.

For the average child medical care has changed, therefore, as a result of the virtual elimination of severe infections, to the immediate treatment of minor problems and, above all, to serious attempts to tackle social and emotional difficulties, for which it is much harder to provide evidence of dramatic 'cures'. You do not 'cure' an IQ of 60, or a truanting child whose father has deserted his mother, or a child who is edgy and awkward and experiments with drugs. Instead you try to make life better for such children and for their families with the help of the doctor, teacher, social worker, and the police or the courts. A host of statutory and voluntary bodies has been set up to support the family, especially the family that has broken up. This is medicine at its most social. It is not hospital medicine: it is social medicine.

What, then, of adults? Apart from birth, death is the most dramatic event of their lives. Between 1904 and 1964 the death rate fell for young adults between the ages of 15 and 44 to about a fifth of what it was. The most dramatic decline took place between 1904 and the end of the Second World War, mostly as a result of the elimination of tuberculosis and certain other infectious diseases. But to balance this dramatic fall in the death rate there was a rise in the incidence of cancer, heart disease and deaths from accidents, especially traffic accidents. Heart disease is the most important cause of young male deaths and cancer of young female deaths.

But death is only a final point in illness: obviously, illness and death are not the same thing. How typical of illness are mortality rates? They are, of course, fairly good indicators of serious illness, because by definition serious illness is related to death, but what do they tell us about everyday aches and pains? If we look at why people actually visit their doctor, we find that the reasons they give bear little or no relation to the final causes of death. In the 1970s for every thousand people the following numbers sought medical treatment in the year (a number of patients are double-counted as they come into several categories):

402	respiratory infection (cold, flu, tonsillitis)
195	injections and check-ups
151	vague symptoms (coughs or pain)
147	psychiatric difficulty (anxiety and insomnia)
142	a disorder of the nervous system, eyes and ears (wax, pink eye)
133	a skin problem (eczema)
109	rheumatism, arthritis and back pain
105	an accident (mostly sprains and cuts)
98	genito-urinary problems (cystitis)
97	stomach upsets and worse
93	infections (including serious diarrhoea)
86	hypertension, heart disease or kidney disease

Of course, all these categories overlap. The number of people who do not consult a doctor at all in a year is surprisingly high, and the number of people who visit their doctors frequently is also high. It seems to be a matter of habit. Much medical treatment, too, is informal: people often treat themselves by trying out well-known remedies like whisky and lemon, or they do what the woman next door suggests.

These figures show that what people consult their doctors about is only rarely the really serious illness: what people die of is usually quite different from what they suffer from while they are alive. Many (perhaps most) visits to the doctor end up with a prescription or a certificate. We know what most prescriptions are for, and they match up with the reasons given for the visits that people pay to the doctor. In 1979, 88 million prescriptions were for sleeping pills, tranquillizers and pain killers; 54 million were for heart disease; 44 million (mainly penicillin) were for infections; 36 million were for coughs, colds and asthma. And so it goes, down to 5 million prescriptions for vitamin preparations.

This avalanche of prescribed medicine is supplemented by proprietary medicines not prescribed by doctors, such as aspirins and tonics bought from the local chemist, and many of those languish in cupboards or are poured down the sink. Half the drugs prescribed are not in fact taken at all or are taken in a 'non-compliant' way. We have already seen in general terms that many of the anti-infective drugs are extremely effective: they offer a cure. But some others do not. In the same way that food is not a cure for hunger in the sense that you crave another meal a few hours later because you are hungry again, so some drugs merely alleviate and some do little or nothing. The effectiveness of medicine for a patient varies. Many drugs are remarkably effective; some patients do not take the drugs properly; and some drugs are unnecessary.

It is worth pursuing this investigation somewhat further. We have already seen that most visits to a doctor are for relatively minor complaints, although they may have tiresome, uncomfortable or embarrassing symptoms. We have seen too that the usual outcome of a visit to the doctor is a prescription for a fairly innocuous drug, which alleviates rather than 'cures' in any radical sense; and we shall show in

17

our discussion of the health service (chapter 9) that the doctor (and the local chemist and the community nurse) is a most effective line of defence for these non-lethal conditions.

If we look at doctors' consultations for the middle-aged (45 to 64), we see that coughs and colds, arms and legs (that is, rheumatism and arthritis) and digestive problems lead the list. Over four out of ten visits to the doctor are prompted by these three conditions. Coughs and colds and bronchitis become more serious for the older patient. The later middle-aged suffer from pneumonia and chronic bronchitis, and some die from them. But among the middle-aged most visits to the doctor are to alleviate coughs and colds, aches and pains and indigestion. Only rarely is death the outcome.

And death, as we learned at the beginning of the chapter, is likely to come to men over 70 and women over 80, through heart disease, cancer and respiratory infections. Appalling diseases like multiple sclerosis do not kill many people. Attempts to find miracle cures for debilitating but non-lethal ailments require research that is costly and disproportionate compared with that for the major causes of death which, if they were controlled, really would affect death rates. People would live longer, and the quality of life would improve.

This chapter has looked at why and when most people die in Britain. In the nineteenth century it was children who died from infections; now it is the elderly who die from heart and lung diseases and from cancer. British children today are rarely severely ill, and the ailments which prompt adults to consult their doctors during their lives are seldom serious either – mostly coughs and colds, anxiety and insomnia. As a country, however, Britain is burdened with medical institutions that were once needed but are no longer apposite. We have too many large old hospitals: hospitals for children, hospitals for infectious diseases, hospitals for those with serious illnesses which once dragged on and on and on. Today different kinds of medical care are more suitable.

The provision of care, as we shall show, now lies principally in the hands of local community institutions, including the general practitioner and his or her team of workers, who have access to modern drugs which prevent, cure and act as palliatives. Hospitals are largely for

18

sophisticated diagnosis, for the costly treatment of a certain number of conditions which require expensive equipment and for the severely ill. Those with chronic illnesses are best treated either at home or in 'homes' – especially the psychiatrically ill and handicapped – and do not need the hospital. The hospital will always be with us, but, as is explained below, its role ought to be very specialized.

Before turning to the three diseases that will in the foreseeable future, continue to call on the technical equipment that is available in hospitals, let us consider the problems that are now confronting the Third World. For the experience of the advanced industrial nations over the last two centuries – the raising of the standard of living, the conquest of bacterial infection, the advent of modern drugs – is being condensed in the Third World into a few decades.

3

Poor Countries

Chapter 2 reviewed the revolutionary change that has occurred in the pattern of recorded morbidity and mortality over the last couple of hundred years in Britain. In the nineteenth century many people died from infectious diseases and children bore the brunt; today most people die from heart, respiratory diseases and cancer, and children seldom die. In extending life expectancy, hygiene, nutrition and environmental improvements have played a large part, larger even than that of medicine, doctors and hospitals. Figures given in chapter 2 also show that the initial effect of improvements in public health and preventive medical care was to create a population expansion. People came to use contraceptives only later, when they were sure that the children to whom they gave birth would live to maturity to have children in their turn.

These same patterns can be seen at work in the Third World today. There infectious diseases are rife, and children pay a heavy toll, just as those of advanced nations did in the nineteenth century; where medical help is available and public health has improved, the population is increasing. But since poorer countries are repeating recognized experiences and are being helped by the knowledge of post-industrial societies, the entire pattern is greatly accelerated: what we went through over 200 years they are undergoing in a much briefer span of time, for they are simultaneously both improving their environment and using the latest drugs, antibiotics, vaccines and immunization procedures.

Infectious diseases are widely prevalent in under-developed countries; it is still the communicable illnesses that kill there. In many poor countries, 40 per cent of deaths among the under-5s are caused by combinations of diarrhoea, pneumonia, influenza and worm infestation. Those who do not die from these illnesses may well be

21

physically and mentally impaired by having caught them in infancy, and they are left vulnerable to other diseases. Measles, for example, causes 200 times as many deaths in the Third World as in developed countries.

In many parts of the Third World, 160 children die for every 1,000 live births, and the true figure in rural areas is probably more likely to be 200 infant deaths for every 1,000 born. (In the United Kingdom in 1970 the figure was 1.1 per 1,000.) The maternal death rate in sub-Saharan Africa is three hundred times that of the United Kingdom. These are horrific figures and seem outrageously unacceptable to us now, although they were commonplace in parts of early Victorian Britain.

Forty per cent of the deaths that occur in under-developed countries are those of children under 5 years of age, a figure very similar to the proportion in Britain in the 1870s. Experts fear, however, that the actual figure may be as high as 80 per cent in some places. The main causes of death are poverty, malnutrition, parasitic infections, gastro-intestinal diseases and pneumonia: the conquest of hunger and infection has yet to be completed in many parts of the world. Indeed, in some of these countries the young experience only a few days' freedom from illness each year and, as a result, are often mentally or physically handicapped on reaching maturity. From our own experience we know that to break such cycles of poverty, malnutrition and disease it is necessary to change environmental and behavioural patterns as well as to provide medicine. Doctors, drugs, hospitals by themselves are not enough. They may help to eradicate hookworm or leprosy, but what is really needed is more nutritious food distributed more evenly through-out the population, better housing, cleaner living conditions, piped water, sewage plants and an altogether healthier environment.

However, history tells us – and indeed it is patently clear now in such countries as Mexico and Nigeria – that improved living conditions will at first lead to a larger proportion of children in the total population: this in turn will increase the level of infectious diseases spreading through those areas which are still overcrowded. Those living in the centres of cities, where public health measures are efficient, may be better off, but those children in the slum and shanty-town areas on the outskirts will still die like flies. Control of population size is, therefore, of great importance.

High fertility is in itself a major cause of ill-health, for bearing one child a year, year after year, exhausts the mother, who then dies early from what is called the 'maternal depletion syndrome'. This in turn means that there are children running around motherless who become ill-fed and are deprived of adult attention and care or who are absorbed into the big families of their relatives to struggle for survival as best they can.

Initially a rapidly growing population increases the socio-economic problems. This means that in cities like Calcutta worse than Dickensian conditions prevail. But before birth-control programmes are acceptable mothers will have to be persuaded that their existing children will survive beyond their earliest years. This is a difficult task because infant mortality rates will not drop until the population stabilizes. Birth control must be encouraged to walk hand in hand with other elements of health care, so that parents can see that the children to whom they give birth really will stand a chance of surviving to old age.

As the first elements of health care begin to take effect, mortality rates for children decrease and initially there is a large population increase: in its turn this expanding population demands health care and education before it will start to control itself and stabilize. Whereas the Western world saw this happen gradually over decades, the Third World is going through the same process at lightning speed; the world population will increase alarmingly over the next few years. Between 1980 and the year 2000 world population is expected to rise from 4,400 million to 6,000 million. Around a quarter of this projected 6,000 million live in the developed world now. By the year 2000 this proportion will become one-fifth. Africa, not China, will experience the largest population boom. China is attempting to achieve zero population growth by the year 2000 by restricting the age of marriage, by encouraging families to have only one child, through widespread education about, and supply of, contraceptives and by offering tax incentives and other inducements to those with only one child. The state makes it quite clear that it is socially unacceptable to have a large family.

China has recognized what some other countries have yet to learn, that people must be socially educated to accept contraception. Women in particular must be encouraged to accept its usefulness and must be educated in its practical advantages. Better education for women will lead to better child health, which in turn will lead to greater acceptance of fertility limitation. In order to accomplish this there must be a more responsible attitude towards women in Third World countries. Unfortunately, poorer countries tend to limit opportunities for women severely; for example, there are often cultural barriers against the education of women; they are left out of group discussions; they are discouraged from participating in many decisions that affect rural and urban life; and in some cases they are even less well fed than men. (In India men have a higher life expectancy than do women.) But population increases will not be curbed unless medical, social and educational care for women in the under-developed countries is much improved: offering them better medical care, higher standards of sanitation and better housing in which to bring up their children would have long-term benefits for the countries concerned.

Life expectancy is on average about eight years less in the Third World than in the West. Many of those adults who do survive can expect to drag out a quarter of their lives in a disabled state; and, most unfortunately, as conditions improve these people will be subject to some of the afflictions that burden elderly people in the West. They too will develop arthritis, circulatory illnesses and cancer – diseases which are new to them.

Standards of nutrition, sanitation, education, housing and the availability of medical service are all affected by the level of economic development. Pure water is much more significant to a community's health than the application of medical therapies after people have become infected. The major health problem of Third World countries is poverty. Because they are so poor some Third World countries devote only 1 or 2 per cent of their Gross National Product (GNP) to medical care, representing in many cases a per capita expenditure of less than $2 a year. First World countries spend more of their larger GNP on health – usually between 6 and 9 per cent. Expenditure from both public and private sources is therefore running at over £300 per capita per year in the richest countries.

24

Inevitably, therefore, expenditure in poor countries is negligible as a proportion of total world health expenditure. The lack of economic resources in the Third World and the consequent effect on health are manifested especially in the urban areas, expanding rapidly because of high fertility within the towns themselves and, as a result of population drift, in shanty towns on urban outskirts. Urban population growth is as high as 10 per cent a year in some African countries. It is impossible to match environmental and health care with such urban development. Money is not being made available for the most elementary needs. Contaminated water supplies and rudimentary sanitation are probably the biggest health problems. Over one-third of the developing countries covered by the UN world economic survey in the late 1960s reported that more than 40 per cent of their urban houses lacked piped water, and the position has altered little since then. The shortage of safe water supplies in developing countries could be met by improving sanitation and sewage disposal. This need not be expensive, but it will require skill. If rural populations are encouraged to use hygienic methods of sewage disposal, a major source of infection would be inexpensively reduced. Perhaps one-third of the babies who die could be saved, as they were in European cities in the last half of the nineteenth century.

Many people in the Third World are short of food. Protein deficiency causes ill-health, associated with under-nourishment. An estimated 60 per cent of the under-developed countries' people are malnourished in some way, while 20 per cent suffer from sheer hunger. (Protein–calorie deficiency diseases include kwashiorkor.) But malnutrition and infection should not be considered separately. Clearly much ill health is due to malnutrition, which reduces the body's resistance and powers to combat disease.

In some developing areas, especially the socialist countries of southern Africa, diet improvement is restricted by absolute shortage, reaching famine scale occasionally, but more generally by difficulties of distribution and by custom. Milk is often not drunk by pregnant women; most food is given to adult males; children are fed on low-protein and low-calorie foods, partly because of scarcity, partly by custom and partly because of insufficient knowledge.

In sum, environmental conditions could be inexpensively improved by simple education in diet and better sanitation, and health could be improved probably more by this than by any other expedient – certainly more than by additional expenditure on medical care. Some medical care is most useful, however. Control of infectious diseases can be achieved by changes in the environment, especially by the purification of water supplies and the elimination of swamps and other breeding places for bilharzia and malaria; by changes in such small things as domestic sanitary behaviour; and by increasing the population's immunity to diseases by vaccination and immunization. Direct medical intervention along these lines has already proved successful.

Until recently malaria was prevalent over wide areas of the earth's surface, but as a result of the use of DDT against the mosquitoes which carry disease, the draining of swamps and stagnant pools which are the mosquito's habitat, education programmes covering the causes of malaria, and the use of preventive drugs, large parts of the world have now become malaria-free. Another indirectly transmitted disease, bilharzia, is also on the wane as a result of education, medical care and the use of an expensive vaccine. Fears were expressed at one point that bilharzia might increase when the Kariba, Upper Volta and Aswan dams were built, as the disease is carried at one point in its lifecycle in snails which like very slow-flowing water, but this does not seem to have been a problem.

Third World countries, as I have explained, have less money than most to spend on medical care. Thus they suffer from an absolute shortage, of medical facilities, and those facilities that are available are all too often confined to the main cities. Distribution of medical resources is often expressed, on paper, in terms of the number of doctors, nurses or hospital beds per head of the population, but such statistics can be misleading if all these resources are in one corner of a country and accessible only to the inhabitants who live in that area. Generally, in the developing countries hospital treatment is available only in the towns: large sections of the rural population must do without. Yet about half of government health expenditure in these countries is devoted to hospital services: about one-third is spent on personal health services, and the remainder is often divided between non-personal public health services and teaching.

The point was made in chapter 2 that five of the great London teaching hospitals were built in the early eighteenth century, yet it was over a hundred years before medical science lowered mortality rates. Although improvements in Third World medicine have accelerated the effects of medical science, the building of hospitals is not the best way to improve a nation's health. The building of large hospital facilities means both that much more money is being spent on those who live in urban than in rural areas, as we have noted, and that too great a proportion of medical expenditure altogether is being invested in too few specialized objectives. Large hospitals attract medical personnel like magnets, and those who train in them all too often wish to remain near them: doctors cluster round the hospitals because they feel that their professional needs are capable of being met only if they have ready access to X-ray machines, scanners, the latest diagnostic tools and specialized operating theatres. Such medical practitioners are often Western-trained, interested in using their professional skills rather than in more practical forms of medical care better suited to under-developed countries. As has been shown, health standards can increase only through improved sanitation, nutrition and decreased fertility, with emphasis on preventive medicine. Hospital research units may discover new drugs, but such Western-style curative units should not be allowed to swallow up so much of the available money. It would be much more appropriate to spend large sums on improving living standards and on changing people's attitudes towards overcrowding, eating, drinking, and contraception – of course, with due regard to the structure of their society and their material and spiritual cultures. India, for example, has pioneered the use of auxiliary workers – often themselves barely more knowledgeable than their neighbours – who have some skill and experience in agricultural, hygiene and medical techniques. Their value is inestimable, and their work is far more useful than that of doctors with sophisticated knowledge and techniques.

In the Third World some countries are developing fast; others have pockets of poverty but are rapidly industrializing. The term covers extremes of culture, physical characteristics, diseases and allied problems, so what is a good solution in one country may be wrong for another. Hence the lessons from the history of medical advancement in Europe cannot be directly applied wholesale to the Third World today. Moreover, it must be remembered that in a typically poor country few resources are available for the 70 per cent or so who live in rural areas.

27

Having taken all the above factors into consideration, however, there are some encouraging signs. In many countries undue pessimism is not called for. India, for example, has made extraordinary progress; Malaysia is barely a Third World country. A baby born in the Third World today will live ten years longer than one born there in 1960. The crude birth rate in Asia, Africa and Latin America has fallen overall by 20 per cent in the past twenty years. Literacy is up from one-third to half of the total Third World population. Smallpox has been eradicated, and malaria, hookworm, leprosy and tuberculosis are much rarer today. The more widespread application of preventive medical techniques should see them nearly wiped out soon. Although it would be foolish to be too optimistic, the figures should be better on all counts by the year 2000.

Non-socialist African countries have rapidly improved their general health status, as have the capitalist economies of Korea, Singapore, Taiwan and Hong Kong. (A man born and brought up in Hong Kong now has a projected life expectancy of 76 years, a figure equalled only by Japan and Sweden.) By contrast, in low-income countries with per capita GNP $400 expenditure on health represented only 1 to 1.5 per cent of GNP in 1979, or an average of $3 per head. These figures represent over half the world's population. For nations with GNPs in the $400 to $4,000 range, the equivalent figures similarly average 1.5 per cent of GNP, or $20 per capita, although in this category there is much more variation; for example, Nigeria spends roughly 0.5 per cent of GNP on health, as does the Yemen, while Brazil allocates more than 1.5 per cent, and so does Singapore. However, these figures do not include private outlays such as direct consumer payments, insurance payments or industry-subsidized health schemes, nor voluntary contributions, armed forces and local government health spending, aid-funded health projects, government payments to mission hospitals or state investments in preventive medical schemes such as sanitation works.

The local communities are spontaneously generating their own health care – obviously, the military and the civil service tend to look after their own, and so do multinational corporations. And there are widespread development projects – for example, irrigation – which have, almost as by-products, raised nutrition and hygiene standards and enabled elementary health care to be introduced. But even so, there are gross differences between what is spent in a very poor country like Ethiopia and what is spent in a comparatively rich one like Malaysia. In 1981 the World Bank concluded that the limited evidence available suggested that in total 'About 6 per cent to 10 per cent of the gross domestic product is spent on health care . . . in the developing countries.' Although exceptions exist, 'Generalizations to the effect that the world's poor nations could as a whole easily and significantly increase their total health spending are of limited validity.'

With their slender financial budgets, therefore, the poorest countries must be helped to concentrate their resources on the most useful and beneficial areas of preventive health care. They should refrain from the inappropriate construction of large, well-equipped teaching hospitals, which many of them built in the 1950s and 1960s; instead they must balance their programmes by aiming to eradicate or control certain diseases and by initiating 'health for all' programmes which concentrate on:

education relevant to health;
the provision of adequate food supplies;
clean water and adequate sanitation services;
maternal and child health care, including family planning;
the prevention and control of endemic diseases;
the provision of a basic range of medicines or 'essential drugs'.

The World Health Organization hopes that by 2000 every country will be devoting at least 5 per cent of its GNP to health; adult literacy will have mounted to at least 70 per cent; average life expectancy will be at least sixty years; and infant mortality will be no more than fifty per thousand live births. In an endeavour to achieve these aims various special programmes have already been launched by the World Health Organization, the World Bank and other aid agencies. There is an Expanded Programme on Immunization; 1980 to 1990 has been made World Water Decade; and a special Action Programme on Essential Drugs has been created.

The major drawback to such programmes, however, is the lack of

29

appropriate health-care infrastructure in many developing countries. There are not enough trained people to carry out plans at the different levels; there are too few medical auxiliaries, staff and basic drugs available at the primary (village) level to get the programmes off the ground; referrals to regional centres are made difficult by lack of transport; and there is weak administration from above.

Nor is it a good idea for outside authorities to intervene in such programmes in order to try to make them more efficient, for excessive intervention from outsiders who do not understand the subtleties of the local people's culture and mores may merely put their backs up and, worse than achieving a little, may be counter-productive. If a Western-trained individual were, say, to arrive at a village to provide a new pure water supply, the local people might well think that he or she was interfering with their long-established customs and even, possibly, with patterns of recreation associated with river water. Great care is needed in explaining to villages the advantages of clean water and the ways in which it can become contaminated; even greater care is required to ensure that the new tap or pipe is placed in a suitable place. Unknown to the Western intervener, dominant local figures may restrict access to water supplies; alternatively, a Westerner may find that he or she has placed the new supply on sacred or taboo land or in a place where the villagers have no right to go.

If primary care systems are introduced aggressively and then fail, a population will be left no better off; indeed, it may be culturally impoverished as well. Even if health is improved, wellbeing may be diminished. It is difficult for Western health workers to see that it may be better to preserve a culture's integrity than swiftly to reduce the number of baby and child deaths. The difficulty is that people cut off from their traditional culture too quickly may lose a way of life that is valuable in itself and become rootless labourers drifting towards unemployment in the shanty towns. It is far better to go more slowly, even though common humanity seems to dictate quick life-saving measures, to enable people's self-respect and dignity to adapt to change.

Where possible, it is productive to work through local people. But perhaps it is even better to try to eradicate a single condition rather than to interfere directly in the lives of the people. It is probably more effective in the long run to try to eliminate guinea worms, which are transmitted through infected drinking water, than to try to provide vast areas with tap water. Indeed, some experts have argued that such diseases as diarrhoeal illnesses, measles, whooping cough, neonatal tetanus and schistosomiasis should be made special targets throughout the world in an effort to wipe them out altogether. These problems can be alleviated by simple services – for example, separating sanitation from drinking water – which do not require an elaborate infrastructure. And a series of simple measures, each one effective, adds up to a major transformation in health.

However, there are those who see the concentration of drug manufacturers on the Third World as 'exploitation'. An organization known as Health Action International has been formed to combat such exploitation. It claims that medicine manufacturers deliberately 'ill-treat' consumers. (A number of Eastern bloc organizations offer similar criticism, although it may be founded on their competition with Western companies for Third World medicinal supplies.) It is felt that unsafe products banned in the West are dumped on Third World countries, that medicine promotion is misleading and that excessive claims are made for products, while side-effects are played down. Prices are also thought to be excessive. Substances involved include chloramphenicol and other antibiotics, treatments for diarrhoea in children, injectable hormonal contraceptives and certain types of analgesics containing amidopyrine and dipyrone.

A large number of modern medicines that are useful primarily for Third World diseases already exist, having been developed by scientific research in the West. Pharmaceutical companies should continue to develop more of these. They should undertake further research to relieve suffering, to find cures and to invent better preventive medicine, especially for those lands which have no manufacturing facilities. They should also encourage those countries which have growing drug industries of their own to manufacture a broad range of bulk drugs and to repack and process these into dosage forms themselves. The Third World needs its own drugs for its own tropical diseases, but to develop them is a difficult and extremely

31

expensive process; it will require great efforts on the part of the Western pharmaceutical industry.

Many of the Third World's health problems were the First World's five or six generations ago: infant mortality at over 200 per thousand babies born, child death rates of fifty per thousand per annum, high mortality from infectious diseases among adults, low life expectancy. In many cases these problems are being overcome first by hygiene and better living conditions and then by drugs. In some instances both aspects of health are being provided simultaneously, which has led to a population explosion. Mass vaccination and immunization, the reduction of child deaths and the decrease in adult deaths, compressed into a much shorter period than in Western experience, has itself brought problems.

Overcrowding, slums, shanty towns, high fertility rates and poverty exacerbate these difficulties. There is a pressing need for contraception. However, bodies like the World Bank and the World Health Organization have provided a great deal of information and a detailed framework for health planning. Effective health care for large numbers of poor people is beginning to be possible. Moreover, the barriers to such health care are now better understood, among them inappropriate training levels and expectations among health workers; the misapplication of medical technologies, especially large hospitals filled with under-used equipment instead of local dispensaries diffused throughout the countryside; expensive cancer remedies in cities; while rural areas lack essential vaccines or pure water supplies.

Great hopes are now pinned on the 'health for all by the year 2000' concept and on sensible programmes which concentrate on key problems, but the beliefs, values, knowledge and behaviour of individuals must change if the guidance of international agencies is to have any significant effect.

It will be clear that the Third World is heterogeneous. Each state of society requires a different medical regime. It is not for the Third World to copy the First World now; it must study our history. And, in the Third World as in the First, medicine is marginal (though crucial) to the main problem – the question of the way of life of the community.

4

The Life Shatterers

This chapter is devoted to three illnesses: heart disease, cancer and mental illness. The first two may be regarded as contemporary epidemics. They are big killers; they are what people fear; and they claim a large part of hospital care. Progress in their diagnosis and treatment will profoundly affect the demand for, and the supply of, medical care. Mental illness, by contrast, is not often lethal, if only because the suicide rate has dropped, but it causes more misery than any other group of illnesses. It is included in this chapter because it is a destroyer of happiness. And, as we shall see, more and more medical care is about making life more tolerable; less and less is concerned with saving life.

Several general lessons can be drawn from this chapter. The question of happiness and a tolerable life cries out for closer examination. We shall see, too, that while medicine – science-based medicine, relying on medical and scientific expertise – has much to contribute once illness has struck, the major problems are how to prevent illness from striking at all and, once it has been treated, how to make life liveable.

Let us turn first to heart disease. Heart disease has been a major killer since the 1930s. It affects middle-aged men especially severely – it is, indeed, the commonest cause of death in middle-aged men. Why has it become so dominant?

A word of caution first. The seeming dominance of heart disease as a killer may be in part a statistical illusion because the evidence for the rise in such deaths is not absolutely clear. As knowledge has advanced, more and more disease is precisely classified, and what were once reported as general illnesses are now coded with more accuracy as heart disease. Doctors have clarified their language; diagnosis has become better; the stethoscope is now backed up by direct examination of the heart itself by inserting a catheter, by the cardiogram, by blood tests; and more and more diagnostic tests are evolved every year. So more heart disease is recognized for what it is than used to be the case. However, only a post-mortem can really reveal the disease from which sombody has died; even then pathologists will differ, perhaps by as much as 10 per cent, in defining the exact cause of death. It may be true to say that fifty years ago heart disease was under-reported. As it has become medically 'fashionable' it may now be over-reported. Moreover, the trend of deaths does not mirror the trend of the disease because treatment has become much more effective. There is more illness than death. Consequently, nobody is exactly sure of the incidence of heart disease behind the apparently horrific figures, though it is certainly extremely high. Enough is known for the main facts to be clear: heart disease is the most prevalent and lethal illness in Britain, and its incidence has increased.

What are the causes of this increase in heart disease? The main causes can be found by means of clinical examination, by reference to scientific theories explaining what the doctors find and by comparing the incidence of the disease between the sexes, different social classes and different nationalities.

Before going on to do this it may be appropriate to say a word about statistics (which, as the saying goes, are less reliable only than lies and damned lies). All statements about cause and effect are statistical statements or, as pointed out in chapter 1, statements about probabilities. Some people survive the most appalling risks; others die of negligible mishaps. But the chances that something risky will happen to all of us are fairly well known, otherwise we would never be able to insure anything. All that 'science' does is to explain the chain of cause and effect. To say that something is 'purely statistical' is like saying, 'It actually happens', though some people tend to think it means, 'We don't know.'

The highest rates of heart disease are found among men rather than women. Among men they occur among Scots, Irish, Welsh and English, white and Indian South Africans and other similar peoples of

34

the advanced world. Rates have been falling in the United States, but it has been found that among those who have traditionally known low rates – for example, Japanese immigrants to California – the incidence rises to American norms. It seems fairly clear, therefore, that some heart disease is a product of the Western lifestyle. But heart disease is not the consequence purely of prosperity because it is much more prevalent among manual workers than among the better-off. For example, non-commissioned officers in the services – drawn largely from the manual working class – have much more heart disease than officers of the same age, drawn from professional groups in the population.

Despite considerable research and clinical effort, the actual causes of heart disease (which represents, of course, a broad spectrum of illness) are yet to be fully understood. As Nick Wells of the Office of Health Economics says:

> Coronary heart disease is the collective term given to various symptomatic manifestations which are the result of injurious processes occuring in the coronary arteries. The latter become narrowed, with consequent impairment of blood flow and hence supply of oxygen to the heart's muscle. These developments may give rise to a spectrum of events, from angina through myocardial infarction to sudden death.
>
> The disease processes involved have yet to be established. Epidemiological investigation has nevertheless uncovered a number of behavioural and other factors which appear to predispose to a greater likelihood of the development of symptomatic illness. Of these, cigarette smoking, elevated serum cholesterol levels and raised blood pressure have emerged as the most significant – together they can increase by eightfold the chances of a 'coronary event'. Estimates suggest that about 20 per cent of men and women aged 30–49 have two or more concurrent major risk factors predictive for the disease.*

*Coronary Heart Disease; The Scope for Prevention (Office of Health Economics), 1982.

The relationship between cigarette smoking and heart disease is very close. One of the reasons why female heart disease rates have risen is because women are smoking more, and one reason why army officers suffer from less heart trouble than NCOs is because they smoke less. The cigarette lobby used to argue that there was no clear clinical evidence associating smoking with disease, that both might in fact share a common cause (say, anxiety), or that particular personality types might be more likely to smoke, and therefore to have heart disease, so that stopping smoking would not have any effect on the incidence of disease. But among those groups that have stopped smoking – doctors, for example – there has been a significant drop in heart disease, so smoking must be a cause. Moreover, the effect of cigarette smoking on disease is greater the more a person smokes, and the risk of disease falls the moment he or she stops smoking. It can be said with certainty that if all cigarette smoking stopped, heart disease would be dramatically reduced.

There is probably a genetic predisposition to one or other of these conditions. It is impossible to calculate the risk factor exactly, but the most reliable current evidence suggests that cigarette smoking is the most serious risk; raised blood pressure is a second; high blood cholesterol is a third. These links can all be proved statistically. It is known that diabetes sufferers are also at risk from heart disease, as are people with a family history of such disease – though family histories of illness are notoriously unreliable. Nevertheless, if your father or mother had heart disease, it is more than likely that you will too.

Research is concentrating on several other risk factors. Obesity, stress, a striving or 'type A' personality, the absence of hard physical exercise and the presence of hard tap water have all been linked with heart disease. Some of these are not independent variables. Someone who overeats and takes no exercise will tend to be fat, and fat people store cholesterol in their fat. Stress and a striving, over-anxious personality are related to high blood pressure. Exercise can reduce stress and blood pressure. A fit person will probably not want to smoke.

So all the likely predispositions to heart disease – apart from the genetic and links with other causes as yet undiscovered – amount to a need to change a lifestyle from an inactive, over-eating, over-smoking set of habits to one based on exercise and moderation. The question of happiness and a tolerable life, of preventing serious illness and making life liveable, could not be more relevant to any illness than it is to heart disease.

Meanwhile, however, hundreds of thousands of people suffer from heart disease. What can be done therapeutically? First of all, much of the pain – which is called angina – can be alleviated or relieved altogether by drugs, notably beta blockers. Blood pressure can be reduced by drugs and by exercise. By-pass surgery – the replacement of blocked arteries – is becoming a major solution to the problem of the reduction of severe illness and death. Nick Wells of the Office of Health Economics says:

It was not until the introduction of the cardio-pulmonary by-pass machine in the 1950s and coronary arteriography in the early 1960s that a direct surgical approach to the coronary artery became feasible. The first successful operation, in which myocardial blood flow was restored by the grafting of a length of reversed saphenous vein between the aorta and the diseased coronary artery beyond its point of occlusion, took place in Texas in 1964.

The Americans have pioneered and led the adoption of this technique, and it is estimated that approximately 110,000 procedures were performed in the USA in 1980. This compares with a figure of approximately 4,500 in England and Wales.*

In America, therefore, the operation is five or six times more common than in Britain, in proportion to the population.

It must be said, however, that experience indicates that an operation is best for those patients who are not very ill, for whom the operation death rate is 1 or 2 per cent; for more severely ill patients the operation death rate is far higher. Moreover, the signs are that the return of illness is to be expected within ten years for the majority

Coronary Heart Disease; The Scope for Prevention (Office of Health Economics), 1982.

of patients who have been operated on, either because the underlying causes have not altered (the patient continues to smoke, for example) or because the operation is not as yet as successful as it will be when more experience has been gained.

The most highly dramatized operations – heart transplants – as yet save few lives, and generally for only a short time. But their real significance, of course, is their importance for research. Organ transplants have become fairly common. They are the result of more extensive biological knowledge and of pharmaceutical advances, as well as of progress in surgical techniques. In other words, the spin-off from these procedures may or may not be important: they are not to be evaluated primarily in relation to heart disease.

The debate about cholesterol is connected both with diet and with the development of drugs designed to reduce cholesterol levels. This is not a simple matter. Nick Wells sums up the matter brilliantly in his OHE study. It has been known for some time that a high serum cholesterol level is associated with heart disease. This high level is related to animal fats (meat, butter, milk, cheese, eggs). It seemed at one time that polyunsaturated fats (margarine, for example, which is based on sunflower oil) might actually reduce the effects of meat and butter eating. Obviously, this infuriated the butter manufacturers and delighted the margarine manufacturers. Recent research seems to show that fish, or 'marine-based diets', are more effective than margarine, not because they are low in saturated fats but because they have high-density hipoprotein, which may (as it were) sweep away cholesterol.

Drugs to counter hypertension are effective but not as effective as exercise, loss of weight and reduction in salt; and in any case it is probable that hypertension, like high cholesterol levels, is to some degree genetic in origin.

In short, it seems that heart disease is now on the way down rather than up, partly because of more effective therapies but mostly because of changing lifestyles. Where treatment has been effective, it has alleviated the symptoms, especially pain, for many victims of heart disease.

Cancer kills half as many people as heart disease, but it is probably more feared, since it seems so curiously evil, 'eating' the patient alive, whereas heart disease is seen (mistakenly) as a sudden death. Cancer is usually thought of as a single disease, but it is several, all having the common characteristic that the cells have turned malignant. Perhaps 'malignant neoplasms' most vividly describes what cancer actually is.

The major carcinogens are known. They are tobacco (especially cigarette smoking), asbestos, coal and other hard particles in dust and probably chemicals, especially in food additives. Excessive sun-bathing causes cancer of the skin, as does repeated abrasion (the rubbing of a breast against a loose dress, for example). Cancer is therefore often avoidable, though shock and worry are also thought to play a part. How a cell begins to malfunction and to multiply without restraint is understood now but not why the restraining system breaks down. This will probably be understood in ten years' time, and then more cancer will be successfully treatable.

As with other diseases, with cancer many of the changes in mortality and in morbidity are due to changes and developments in diagnostic techniques. Death rates, moreover, are not an indicator of the incidence of the disease, as we saw in the case of heart disease. The biggest male killer is lung cancer (although numbers are declining, probably because of the drop in cigarette smoking), and the biggest female killer is cancer of the breast. For women cancer of the skin and ovary has grown in incidence, as has lung cancer. Intestinal, stomach and cervical cancer are also killers, although the numbers of the first two are down, perhaps because of dietary changes. Both sexes show a rise in the number of adults dying from leukaemia, which is a form of cancer, and also in those dying from cancer of the pancreas. In England and Wales there has been a cancer registration scheme since 1945. The ten most common sites for cancer in 1977 (expressed as a percentage of all sites) are shown in table 1 (p. 38).

It used to be the case that early diagnosis was not necessarily a help in cancer cases, since much treatment was ineffective. This is no longer true. Childhood leukaemia, for example, once killed all who got it. That is far from being the case now if it is diagnosed early enough. Early mastectomy (removal of part or the whole of the breast), for

Table 1   *The ten most common sites for cancer in men and women, 1977*

Sites of cancer	% of total
Men	
All sites	100
Trachea, bronchus and lung	29
Other malignant neoplasm of skin	11
Prostate	8
Stomach	8
Large intestine, except rectum	6
Bladder	6
Rectum and rectosigmoid junction	5
Pancreas	3
Oesophagus	2
Other and unspecified urinary organs	2
Other	20
Women	
All sites	100
Breast	23
Other malignant neoplasm of skin	10
Large intestine, except rectum	9
Trachea, bronchus and lung	8
Stomach	6
Ovary, fallopian tube and broad ligament	5
Rectum and rectosigmoid junction	5
Cervix uteri, excluding *in situ*	4
Other malignant neoplasm of uterus	4
Pancreas	3
Other	23

Source: Cancer statistics (registrations), Office of Population Censuses and Surveys, 1977 (1982).

example, and early treatment of cervical cancer have undoubtedly decreased the likelihood of the spread of the disease to other parts of the body. Early removal of small malignancies – lumps seen on the body at regular check-ups – have also dramatically reduced the spread of cancer to other sites. It seems that operations for bowel cancer and for the older man's type of cancer (cancer of the prostate) are markedly successful, though it is not known for certain how rapidly these cancers would spread if untreated.

The rate of 'cure' of cancer has improved because of surgery, deep-ray therapy and other chemotherapy developments, but the breakthrough in cancer therapy is still awaited. It is almost certain to arise because of developments in cellular biology and immunology, as the latest research has shown.

Cancer is a 'family' of diseases, of which many members are curable. Much cancer is avoidable. It is a question of lifestyle: a happier and more tolerable life would certainly prevent a great deal of illness, especially if cigarettes were given up and diet was altered; and making life more liveable would remove the need for treatment. Thereafter once cancer has developed it is for the most part treatable.

The other great scourge which leads to hospitalization and, as we have seen, takes up a large part of the time of general practitioners is psychiatric illness. It is absurd to regard all people who suffer from mental distress as psychiatrically ill and in need of treatment, but certain forms of anxiety can be acutely distressing and socially disabling. When these are prolonged, or when an individual seems to lose his or her ability to perceive the world in the same way as the majority of people (as in the case of schizophrenia), it is justifiable to conclude that he or she is mentally ill.

In recent years two major changes have taken place in the care of the mentally ill. The first is that more and more people who are anxious, unhappy or distressed seek medical help and are given psychotropic medication in the form of sleeping pills, tranquillizers, valium and other drugs which alleviate their misery. These can be seen as mere substitutes for the alcohol and opium given at other times and in other places, and the doctor can be regarded in some degree as having replaced the clergyman as a source of talking care; whichever way you look at the development, its effect is positive, comforting and helpful.

The second major change is the emptying of many of the long-stay mental hospitals. Though the number of admissions has not fallen, the length of stay has, because the use of drugs and other techniques has led to more rapid recovery for many patients, and there has been a growing emphasis upon the care of the mentally ill patient in the community.

In 1961 there were 165,000 occupied beds in mental hospitals and psychiatric wards in the United Kingdom. The number of discharges and deaths was 176,000. In other words, the average stay was rather less than a year, which means that, discounting people who stayed for a short time, two decades ago the average mental patient was in hospital for years, possibly for life. The number of occupied beds in 1979 was 100,000 and discharges and deaths totalled 218,000 – that is, the average stay was less than six months, and the rate is still falling.

In the case of mental handicap there were 53,000 occupied beds in 1961 and 55,000 in 1981, but here again the rate of discharge has risen from 10,000 to 25,000 – length of stay is four times longer on average than for mental illness.

Three major sinks have yet to be drained, however: the hospitals full of the senile, the mentally handicapped and the chronically ill, such as psychopaths. For their problems treatment has not yet been found.

Though great efforts are being made on behalf of each of these three groups and there is a growing emphasis on community care for them too where possible, there is likely to be a steady need for such institutions for some long time to come. However, exactly who has to use them and who does not depends a great deal on the community, the individual and the available ancillary services. In this sector of psychiatric disorder there is considerable overlap between domiciliary care and institutional care, and again between institutional care and health care. For example, a senile elderly person may live with his or her daughter, or in an old person's home, or in a psychiatric hospital. Exactly where he or she is depends upon whether or not the daughter can cope, whether the local area has good home help and other services to offer, whether or not there is a community home or nursing home for the elderly in the area, and also upon the degree of senility. Incontinence is frequently the stage at which family and community care ceases. Similarly, depending on the degree of the handicap and the care available locally, someone who is mentally handicapped may live at home, backed up by help from the social services; in community care; or at a school, sheltered workshop, colony or hospital. The psychopath too may be in prison or at large in a hospital or in a part-time sheltered community home or in a long-term institution for the insane.

It is no longer necessary to admit large numbers of patients to hospital. Progress in psychiatric care has improved with the rise of pharmaceutical products that affect the mind and the personality. Many people today can live in the community or at home if they take specific drugs. Reference is sometimes made to the medicines, easily prescribed and casually taken, that are awash in the community, but people underrate the difficulties that are being alleviated. Not only are such drugs helping the anxious, the depressed and those who are unable to sleep but they are also enabling a great many people to remain with their families and to live relatively normal lives instead of being shut up behind walls. It is striking that the expenditure on research into mental illness and on geriatrics is only a tiny fraction of what is spent on cancer. Yet over half of hospital beds are for geriatrics and those suffering from mental handicap and psychiatric illness. As chapter 9 shows, if all these patients could be 'de-hospitalized', the number of occupied hospital beds would be only two-fifths of what it now is.

Drugs are not the only way of dealing with mental illness. There are also psychotherapeutic, psychoanalytical and psychological cures. Opinions differ about their effectiveness, both in diagnosis and in treatment, but it is undoubtedly true to say that information disseminated by psychologists and psychoanalysts has removed mental illness from the category of madness and placed it in that of treatable illness. The research that these people have done and the attitudes and ideas they have taught have spread into the world of the social researcher and the social worker. Through their findings it is now possible both to ensure that social life is less likely to lead to mental illness and to increase the degree of support that anxious and depressed people receive. For example, it has long been known that single people in bedsitters in big cities are far more prone to suicide than others.

Many jobs are stressful. No doctor alone can do much about either, but social agencies can.

Considerations such as these affect the numbers of people seeking treatment. Some radical psychiatrists regard mental illness as non-existent. It is, according to them, a way of labelling an unacceptable lifestyle. According to other radicals, illness is a result of alienation, itself a result of capitalism; hence the way in which the USSR treats dissidents by putting them in psychiatric hospitals, since dissidence there is defined as madness. So here again medicine is a solution to a problem raised by lifestyle. Of course there *is* such a thing as mental illness, but it is often 'illness' in a special sense, and it is not obvious that the doctor is always the right person to treat it.

As knowledge of mental illness has grown, so older physical methods of treatment such as insulin coma, electro-convulsive therapy and cold-water baths have virtually disappeared. The drug revolution is still in its early stages, but already there are many important drugs that alleviate really serious mental disorders. Their effect will be to allow more people to leave long-stay hospitals and to decrease even further the time that patients spend in short-term hospitals. They may still need to visit hospital occasionally for observation and assessment, but less and less frequently.

The rising incidence of these three major modern life shatterers, heart disease, cancer and psychiatric illness, can be attributed partly to a process of discovery and the redefinition of conditions that existed before but were treated differently (or not treated at all); partly, as in the case of heart disease, there has been a genuine increase. The diseases are not yet curable, but the suffering they cause can be alleviated, the pain lessened and their drastic nature moderated. At the moment these three diseases all take up a great deal of medical time and space, but this will change as treatment by a growing battery of scientific and technological methods and drugs becomes more wide-spread.

High-technology medicine, the theme of chapter 5, will be essential to the understanding and treatment of these 'diseases of civilization', as they are sometimes called – as of many others. It will involve a great deal of research and will be very costly, at least initially. Gradually, as procedures are routinized, as the drugs and equipment are mass-produced, costs per patient will fall. Eventually, as the psychiatric data have shown, hospitals will empty except for the purposes of diagnosis and radical treatment. With the aid of preventive medicine there will be far fewer patients; moreover, in the case of heart disease, cancer and mental illness changes in lifestyle, in habits and in attitudes will do more to control the diseases than will any expensive item of equipment.

5

High-Technology Medicine

Modern medicine is two or three generations old. Florence Nightingale initiated changes in nursing methods; Lister introduced antiseptics; effective anaesthesia started with Clover and Hewitt; X-rays began with the Curies. Then in the 1930s came the great breakthrough: the control of infections with sulphanilomides. This was followed by barbiturates and penicillin. Other revolutionary pharmacological innovations enabled new anaesthetic techniques to be developed, which in turn opened the way to modern surgery.

High-technology medicine involves X-rays, scanners, modern anaesthetics and modern drugs; without these all the paraphernalia of the latest hospital or clinic would be useless. But high-technology medicine is more than that. Nowadays even a doctor alone in the bush, without equipment, is able to focus his skills on the diagnosis of quite complex diseases and illnesses because his high-technology training has taught him how disease processes work, which symptoms they show at various stages and why they do this. He may not be able to treat the patient there and then, but he knows what to look for, how to interpret what he finds and what should be done. The gap between a modern doctor and his grandfather is far greater, therefore, than that between his grandfather and one practising in the eighteenth century. The recent gap represents a radical change in the depth and scope of knowledge of diseases and how they present themselves. High-technology medicine is now just a range of medical adjuncts: it is a breakthrough in understanding.

Without high-technology medicine, then, there would be virtually no modern medical expertise. But there is much criticism of the excessive application of science and technology to illness. Why?

First, it is thought that emphasis upon the scientific side of medicine has tended to diminish the human loving care that doctors and nurses give to their patients. Second, it is argued that an inappropriate proportion of resources is devoted to treating a few patients with uncommon diseases, while others – for example, the elderly and the mentally handicapped – are relatively neglected. Third, the claim is made that the emergence of modern high-technology medicine is a result of a combination of high-cost experimental science (finding out, for example, whether the transplant of an organ is possible at all) and of high-pressure business on the part of the pharmaceutical industry. In short, 'natural' medicine, it is felt, has been replaced by 'high-tech' at the expense of human values and proper priorities. Fourth, it is asserted that much modern medical treatment is unnecessary, a result of demand generated by advertising. As the figures for consultations with general practitioners show (see p. 16), this is an exaggeration. As we shall see from the figures for hospital usage given below, a high proportion of hospital beds is still used for non-high-technology medicine, notably for long-stay patients.

All these arguments rest upon a misconception of what high-technology medicine actually is. The first great pharmaceutical revolution – largely achieved by now – was concerned partly with the control of infection and partly with psychotropic medicines and the control of specific diseases. The initial costs of treatment included the overhead costs of the research effort that enabled these developments to take place. As output grew, so unit costs diminished; each course of penicillin, for example, is now cheap and saves substantial medical costs that would be incurred if penicillin were not available. Medical research of this kind is now being directed towards less common diseases. Inevitably, the high on-costs have to be spread over fewer patients, making each course of treatment seem expensive. On the other hand, those patients who are being treated successfully are not costing money in other ways – they are not taking their GPs' time, making use of hospital beds, taking time off work and so on; and as the decades pass and more and more patients will be treated in the same way, so the costs will be spread more and more widely in time.

The second pharmacological revolution is now under way and will affect cancer, heart disease and respiratory infections – that is to say, major diseases for which initial treatment costs will be high but whose long-run costs will fall dramatically as the overhead is spread over millions of cases.

The same is true of surgery. A complex operation – say, heart-bypass surgery – is accompanied initially by low success rates and high intensive-care costs and requires rare surgical skills, but as the technique is refined, so it becomes more common, the success rate climbs and the cost per case declines. Thus, while high-technology medicine is, by definition, never cheap – because as soon as it becomes cheap it is no longer high technology but ordinary medicine – its cumulative effect is the treatment of many cases that, to all intents and purposes, were formerly not treated at all and to reduce the costs per course of treatment.

Inescapably, as new services are offered so a larger portion of people's income is spent on them, whether directly or by taxation. I use the word 'inescapably' deliberately. If something new comes along to meet a need, people will buy it. One obvious example is refrigerators, which have largely replaced larders. Another is radio and television; no money was spent on either in 1914, yet now hundreds of millions of pounds are spent each year on these two mainstays of contemporary life. People will pay for new products that they find desirable. These products are usually expensive at first. In the case of medicine, however, there are consequences that ultimately reduce costs in the longer run – that is to say, they remove the need for medical care for people suffering from chronic sickness, and they probably offer certain economic benefits, in that the labour force is increased by the reduction in sickness and death.

As will be argued, however, it is a little phoney to present the case for new medicines in terms of economic savings. The case is predominantly humanitarian. For example, a new therapy that permitted elderly people to be more mobile would not make any contribution to the economy, but it would make many people more comfortable and happier, an end that is surely desirable in itself and one for which people will pay. Similarly, cures for dreaded diseases, even though they may kill only a few people each year, are eagerly sought, and society is prepared to pay for the research. A 'cure' for multiple sclerosis, for example, may be very expensive but it is nevertheless desirable. As any disaster shows – whether a ship foundering in a storm or men trapped in a coalmine – the expense involved in rescue attempts is not counted. The implicit value placed on each life saved may run into millions of pounds, but the cost is thought worth while. (Paradoxically, of course, people are apparently unwilling to pay the costs of avoiding major killers such as road accidents, smoking and drinking.)

High-technology medicine falls into two parts; surgery and pharmaceuticals. The first, surgery, is associated with a conception of the hospital as the central medical facility. High-technology surgery now involves a surgeon and his team, anaesthetics, intensive care, blood transfusion, laboratory services, including tissue culture – all taken for granted by a modern sawbones. By contrast, pharmaceuticals uses the hospital primarily as a laboratory (to test blood and so on), and the treatment is generally domiciliary; in most cases the patient lives at home and leads a life that is to some degree normal.

A major effort in basic scientific research has been transmitted to hospitals and general practitioners through a technologically very advanced industry. This enormous effort is a product of the work of the past three generations. New pharmaceutical products have eliminated many childhood diseases; they have reduced the length and number of hospital stays; they have reduced the number of patients in psychiatric hospitals who are suffering from neuroses and psychoses; they have made substantial progress with anti-inflammatory and anti-ulcer therapies, so that the incidence of serious arthritis and stomach complaints has been reduced; and there have been advances in anti-cancer drugs, in anti-viral agents, in pain controllers and in drugs to reduce blood pressure. Of the 2.5 million surgical operations now performed in this country every year, most could not be completed successfully without modern pharmacology.

The idea of high-technology medicine is thus far more complex than might be supposed. High technology has been the cutting edge of a massive change in medicine and a tremendous rise in its effectiveness. Surgery is hospital-based, while medicine is GP-based. The shift in the relative importance of these two sectors is our next theme.

In recent years the number of hospital beds has fallen sharply. In 1980, of 370,000 beds 226,000 were occupied by psychiatric and geriatric patients. If these largely chronic cases are omitted from the calculation, there are about 170,000 beds in use, of which 24,000 are obstetric and gynaecological, 55,000 are medical, 65,000 are surgical and the rest are acute psychiatric, etc. Within this category the length of hospital stay has been shortening, so that in 1980 there were over 1 million patients who spent time in medical beds (that is, each bed was occupied twenty times a year) and over 2 million people in surgical beds (that is, each bed was occupied thirty times a year).

The figures for hospital out-patient visits have been rising – from 40 million in 1955 to over 50 million in 1980. About a quarter of these were accident and emergency cases, indicating the role of the hospital in serious or potentially serious cases. But most attendances are for tests ordered by local doctors or for routine surveillance and follow-up.

Although the number of beds occupied has declined, bed usage has increased substantially. It may seem paradoxical, therefore, to see that waiting lists have also increased. But waiting lists are a fairly steady proportion – about 12 per cent – of the total number of admissions to hospital. Emergencies and serious cases are usually attended to more or less at once; it is the routine cases – predominantly 'cold surgery' (varicose veins and the like) – that are placed on a waiting list. Expressed as a period of time, the delay is about six weeks. Of course, in over-provided specialities there may be no waiting list, whereas in those where demand has outstripped supply the waiting list can be long. An interesting recent study of hip replacement by the Office of Health Economics shows not only that there is a pronounced regional variation in the availability of specialities, but also that in growing departments where spectacular advances are being made (especially surgery) the demand can be met only by rapid switches of personnel and facilities. In the absence of a price mechanism to ensure that this occurs, the health-care authorities are left with a major administrative problem. In consequence, the allocation of resources in the hospital service is the outcome of the interaction of what is available – a historical legacy – and conflicting pressure for resources on the part of the consultants as demand changes. For example, tuberculosis has virtually vanished and heart surgery has arrived; to run down the one and to build up the other is a matter of Health Service politics.

While hospital discharges rose from 5.7 million in 1966 to 7 million in 1980, the total number of beds occupied daily in both 'acute' and 'chronic' hospitals declined from 472,000 in 1961 to 370,000 in 1980. The number of occupied beds in 'acute' hospitals was 170,000, as we have noted, and the average length of stay of medical patients in such hospitals fell from 18.6 to 10.6 days and of surgical patients from 10.7 to 7.8 days. Table 2 indicates the diseases and conditions for which the 170,000 'acute' beds were mostly used.

The cases in hospital are only the tip of an iceberg of medical treatment, most of which is experienced at home. We have already seen that the iceberg itself is only partly representative of illness in society. In Britain we have a hospital system that operates approximately 250 medical, surgical and acute psychiatric beds per parliamentary constituency — say, for towns such as Oxford, Cambridge or Darlington, or half a London borough. A typical modern hospital has between 400 and 800 beds; if all hospitals were on this scale, there would be one hospital catering for every three parliamentary

Table 2   *'Acute' beds: conditions, number occupied and length of stay, 1979*

Condition	No. of beds occupied	Length of stay (days)
Cerebrovascular disease	18,283	60
Injury and poisoning	16,025	11
Malignant neoplasm	14,677	14
Respiratory diseases	14,356	14
Bronchitis, etc.	2,619	12
Diseases of the digestive system	10,976	9
Musculoskeletal disease	10,411	17
Diseases of the nervous system	9,082	36
Pulmonary and heart disease	7,182	21
Ischaemic heart disease	6,071	15

Source: Hospital In-Patient Enquiry 1979, Central Statistical Office, 1980.

constituencies, or about 220 'acute' hospitals in the United Kingdom. In fact, of course, few hospitals are modern, and many towns and counties require smaller hospitals because of sparse populations and long distances. In addition, there will be as many beds for geriatric and chronic psychiatric cases.

To address the questions of whether this provision is at about the right level, whether many smaller hospitals would be more suitable and whether it is, in fact, possible to remove the chronic long-stay patients from the purview of the hospital system altogether, we must first look at what hospitals do — again, recalling that we are talking about 'acute' hospitals only.

At the moment the hospital is organized around the consultant and his or her facilities, particularly the X-ray unit, radiology, haemotology and other testing of biological material, the pharmacy, operating theatres and intensive care units, all of which are represented by heavy fixed costs that cannot be duplicated easily or cheaply. Both in-patient and out-patient services are based on this complex technology. While some of the simpler procedures — routine X-rays and tests, for example — can be located in smaller units, the concentration of expensive equipment and, even more, of the teams of people capable of using it requires a substantial throughput of patients in order to ensure its optimum usage. Clearly, such a concentration of patients requires in turn a sophisticated management system, running all the equipment, organizing the staff and booking the patients, as well as a substantial 'hotel operation' for the staff and students. An 800-bed hospital, with a full-out-patient load, may well employ more than 5,000 people. It is this concentration of people that in the absence of good management, taxes managerial skills, leading to low productivity, high costs and demoralization.

Health Service hospitals do not have budgets in the commercial sense: resources — doctors, other staff — are allocated to them. These resources are felt to be inadequate. The pressure therefore is to acquire more staff, not to fit expenditure to income. Thus in 1979 there were 962,000 people working in the hospital and community health services, of whom 544,000 were medical and nursing personnel; the others were clerks, porters, cleaners and caterers. A large proportion of this million or so people work in 'acute' hospitals. If hospitals were paid by the case and had to keep down the costs of those cases, then the emphasis would be on reducing the number of staff. Instead within a limited NHS budget – but not limited in an effective sense for any hospital – there is pressure to employ more staff and to pay each member badly. The number of staff has risen as the number of beds has fallen. If only productivity could be raised, efficiency (and hence service to patients) would rise as well. A hospital employing 5,000 people has approximately 200 doctors, 2,500 nurses, 350 ancillary workers (pharmacists, radiologists), 600 clerical staff and 1,250 domestics, porters and maintenance people. To run so diverse a group requires considerable managerial skill. The rise of staff levels tends to be lavish, without the constraints of strict budgeting. For this reason the desirability of trying to direct technological advances in order to minimize the scale of the work that has to be done is overwhelming. The more the microchip, for example, and communication devices can enable decentralization to take place, the lower the administrative costs. At present the inefficiencies of large hospitals adversely affect the health-care system. From 1949 to 1980 the number of people working for the National Health Service doubled from 400,000 to nearly 1 million. The greater part of this rise was represented by increases in hospital staff: the number of hospital nurses rose from 147,000 to 318,000, clerical staff from 25,000 to 105,000. The hospital service is the largest and fastest growing part of the NHS, as it is of all modern health-care systems in terms of employment. Even taking into account those who are employed in looking after long-stay patients, the 'acute' general hospital is still the major part of health-care expenditure. Inescapably, it becomes the focus of attention. This concern is accentuated, of course, by the fact that the training of doctors, nurses and paramedicals is for the greater part concentrated on the hospital. Modern medicine has a hospital bias, which in part gives it its high-technology image – in the pejorative sense.

The revolution in medicine has enabled more illnesses to be treated. The case load has therefore risen. Efficiency of treatment has reduced the in-patient population, and the hospitals treat a smaller proportion of illness than formerly. The treatment is more effective, and it is also skill- and capital-intensive. A hospital is an increasingly expensive place to run for that reason alone, but it is also expensive because it employs a great many unskilled, poorly paid staff, whose productivity is low. Therefore the hospital is both more important than it used to be, because it is where the revolutionary advances begin, and less important because one of the consequences of the revolution is that much more illness can be treated sucessfully at home. This requires more staff and resources in primary care, so the urgent need is to make hospitals more efficient and to divert resources to primary care.

According to political propaganda, the hospital is the centre of the Health Service. In part, as we have seen, this view is correct; nevertheless, it is a misleading image in view of the fact that the bulk of medical consultation and care takes place outside the hospital. Non-hospital care is usually defined as the remit of the family doctor, but it is far more than that – it involves community nurses, physiotherapists, pharmacists, dentists, opticians, all of whom deal with far more patients in a year than the hospital service does.

Much discussion has focused on the changing role of the family doctor. The nature of the practice of primary medical care is ill-defined. In 1948, when the National Health Service was set up, the first priority was to provide the mass of sick people with hospital services. As technology and social developments have helped to relieve illness, the NHS has been able to deal with less serious conditions, to specialize in preventive health care that does not require hospital doctors.

Modern medicines, vaccines and antibiotics have enabled many diseases to be contained adequately by the primary health team, which is best able to appreciate the medical needs of people within the community in relation to their family, home and working background. Support is provided by general practitioners, other primary health-care workers like nurses, home helps, health visitors, pharmacists, dentists and the social services, which enable sick people to lead reasonably normal lives – going to work, carrying on family life – rather than confining them to a hospital ward. The possibility of care at home is especially important for children.

This context of primary medical care has now been extended even further, and in an entirely different direction, by fundamental changes in what society expects from its health service. The conception of illness, the kind of conditions that demand medical care, have become considerably extended. Alcoholism, depression, behavioural and mental disorders can now be treated by the medical services.

These changes can be seen by looking at the numbers of general practitioners in the community. In 1948, when the National Health Service was inaugurated, primary care had a second-rate status, and hospitals dominated. Between 1949 and 1971 the proportion of doctors in general practice under the NHS fell steadily as a result. Even in 1968 two doctors, Fry and Mackenzie, could write of the 'low morale' of GPs who felt themselves to be separated from mainstream medicine. Then came innovations stressing the importance of the psycho-social causes of illness and the therapeutic potential of the doctor–patient relationship; as a result, the numbers of doctors working in the community grew. At the same time the numbers working in group practices also increased.

The influence here was the 1966 Doctors' Charter, which encouraged general practices that were better equipped and better managed. This development has gone further in other countries, but even in Britain the figures are impressive: in 1959 31 per cent of practitioners worked single-handedly in England and Wales; by 1970 this total had fallen to 21 per cent. In addition, the number of health centres increased tenfold between 1967 and 1972. By 1980 the health centre was common, and most doctors worked in groups, helped by ancillary staff, who saved the time and increased the efficiency of GPs and provided a full service of nursing care, prescribing, tests, physiotherapy and group work for the elderly. There have been other marked changes: now the GP rarely visits acutely ill people in their own homes; instead chronic patients come to the surgery or health centre, occasionally brought by Health Service ambulances. Further, doctors perform little minor surgery these days, even in rural areas, but instead refer such work to hospital casualty departments.

High technology medicine has reduced the number of beds occupied in hospitals, but those that exist are used more often, although for a shorter time. The number of staff looking after those fewer patients and fewer beds has increased enormously, largely because of the inefficient use of untrained domestic staff. High-technology medicine has also enabled more people to be treated at home by their doctors; it has increased the speed at which they can leave hospital after an operation; it has reduced the number going into hospital in the first place. But it has also increased the number of out-patients and the number of patients visiting hospitals for tests. It has increased the number of ill in the local community who are able to enjoy successful treatment. This growth in the number of ill at home has coincided with an expansion of the miseries and disorders that now come under the doctor's care because he can do something about them. To cope with all this the number of doctors in general practice has risen from 18,000 in 1949 to 23,600 in 1980, while the number of community nurses has trebled.

High-technology medicine has therefore changed the emphasis and intensity of heath care. The hospitals deal with more severe cases but with decreasing numbers of patients in bed, while the doctors and their ancillary helpers have a great many more treatable patients. The number of all medical personnel has increased: there are many more GPs but even more hospital service workers. Do we really need all those huge hospitals, or are they now white elephants? Are they in the right places? Should they be so richly staffed? Modern health care is concerned with the organization of a system to meet changing patterns of demand; in the next chapter I shall look at how Britain is meeting this challenge.

6

The Effects of Change

In two later chapters I look at the structure of the National Health Service in the United Kingdom and the system of health care in other European countries. They vary, of course, and it is easy to set out the abstract theoretical advantages and disadvantages of each from the point of view of a preference for state planning, state ownership, free enterprise or whatever. But important though such theoretical discussion undoubtedly is, theory has always to be perceived operating in the world of the actual. In health care the pace of change has been so rapid that the nature of the problems has altered constantly.

In this chapter, therefore, I discuss the nature of some of the problems that change has created in health care now: the need to expand places offering new forms of treatment, to close redundant facilities, to increase environmental and preventive health measures and to take positive action on many fronts – in industry, at work, in the home, over diet and in the fields of geriatric, psychiatric and social medicine. The scope of health care today and the demands likely to be placed upon health-care resources in the foreseeable future (say, the next thirty years) must be discussed before we look at how they are to be financed and organized.

In the comparatively recent past most medical care had little, if any, positive outcome. The purpose of the doctor and the nurse was to succour and relieve pain, to ease childbirth, to watch at deathbeds, to offer advice and comfort. But in this century, as I have explained, medical care has been transformed by scientific and technological advance, and as the standard of living has risen people have demanded more and better medical care, even in the old-fashioned and literal sense of being looked after.

The initial impact of modern medicine was to cause an explosion in the demand for health care and in its cost. In 1948 the Labour Government in Britain introduced the National Health Service. It dealt predominantly with the control of infection – as in the case of tuberculosis – and with chronic conditions. Its cost was so high that its demands on the state's finances played a major part in the defeat of the Labour Party in the general election of 1951. There has been a constant struggle since then between demand and the cost of health-care provision. And since then the revolution in medicine has swept on.

As a result, many facilities have become redundant. Psychotropic drugs have substantially reduced the number of beds required in psychiatric hospitals; the virtual elimination of tuberculosis has made sanatoria redundant; high-technology medicine has enabled many more to be cared for within the community by their local general practitioners; the concept of illness, of the kinds and conditions which demand medical care, has become more comprehensive; the numbers of beds used in hospitals has fallen, as has the time spent in hospital. On the other hand, the rise of heart disease and cancer has created new demands for medical care; the use of out-patients' facilities has increased; and there are still many long-stay hospital patients with illness for which cures have not yet been found. This changing pattern of demand creates different problems of supply from those caused by a single fall or rise in demand for an existing pattern of supply, especially where there are long lead times, as in the case of medicine; the building of hospitals and the training of doctors, for example, are lengthy processes. The nature of medical care must adjust to the demands made of it, and there is no doubt that institutions involved in the free market can adjust more quickly and easily than those run by the state.

I suggest that the free market can be useful. But the state has a major role to play, and the problem remains: how is health care to be organized and how is it to be financed? It is an almost inescapable fact that any organization will deal with yesterday's problems; it is essential but painful to bring the health-care system up to date. The thesis of this book is that organization should be diverse and decentralized and that financial sources should be widened to include state, insurance and personal spending.

Change occurs rapidly in business. An analogy can be drawn

between health care itself and the industry that has caused much of the change, pharmaceuticals, itself an industry virtually created since the mid-1930s by scientific and technological research.

The pharmaceutical industry is also running an expensive and exceedingly risky business. The time span between the original development of a drug and its successful marketing may be fifteen years – and the time is getting longer not shorter – yet the free-enterprise system has coped highly efficiently with such difficulties. New drugs are produced and sold every year. The industry has met every challenge – too successfully indeed, judging by the industry's critics, who allege that its profits are far too high. But pharmaceuticals are the basis of modern medicine, and all are produced by private-enterprise firms. So it is not inconceivable that medical care itself could be privately financed.

Somehow it will be necessary to come to terms with the need for fewer hospitals, spread more conveniently throughout the community, with their high-technology machinery run by fewer people. Their use will have to be streamlined so that the out-patient facilities and the short-stay beds become more economical. Long-stay hospitals will also have to be updated, rationalized, made more efficient and so handled that they can adapt to changing needs as medical knowledge advances.

At present the way that this issue is tackled is by drawing up regional plans, but the vested interests of existing hospitals delay their closure, and problems of finance prevent the opening of new, smaller hospitals. There is no easy solution; but first of all the public will have to be convinced that hospital care is declining as proportion of the total health-care system, and arrangements will have to be made to ensure that resources are directed from one sector to another, arrangements that will enlist public support rather than arousing antagonism. It will be suggested later that one way to do this would be to organize a part-simulated and part-genuine market system.

As I have explained in previous chapters, general health care in the community will also have to be revitalized. Would it be more sensible to have more group practices? Could some of these take over from hospital out-patient departments? Are we getting the balance right between medical facilities available in the community and in expensive hospital centres?

These are largely matters of finance. If £x were allocated per case treated and the money went to the agency which did the work, then provided each agency (hospital or medical centre) had a budget, the pressure for change would be harnessed to expansion where need was perceived.

Environmental health measures must also be included in considering health care as a whole. Many such measures are now provided free by public health authorities, but they have strong medical connotations. Pure tap water has eliminated cholera; the Clean Air Act has substantially reduced deaths from chronic bronchitis; the monitoring of asbestos works has reduced the incidence of asbestosis. Action by public health authorities and factory inspectors is essential to the preservation of a general level of good health: its costs and financial burdens must be taken into account if the way in which we pay for health is not to make us pay too much for less necessary care – say, the treatment of asbestosis – than for more necessary preventive care. Nobody has yet devised a system for paying for environmental health except through the taxpayer. There is therefore always a tendency to spend too little on environmental health, because it means more public finance without any (immediate) political benefits, such as those that spring from more hospital beds.

The whole conspectus of health care is thus widening, and newer treatments are also increasingly available. How is all this to be paid for? If by insurance, what sort of insurance? Through the state or through private institutions? Should payment for routine medical care be differentiated from payment for sudden, grave or fatal illness?

When discussing payment for health care it is important to bear in mind that illness is associated with poverty and with loss of income. The poor are by and large less healthy than the well off, and indeed illness itself is one of the causes of poverty. If someone is taken ill his or her income tends to fall or to cease altogether, and expenses increase. The better off can mitigate this problem by insurance; the poor cannot afford insurance. For that reason much medical care has either been charitable or provided free at low cost by the state. There seems to be

an irreducible minimum level of free health care in any community –
that offered to the chronically sick, the grossly mentally and physically
handicapped, the senile, who in the end are almost inevitably the
responsibility of public authorities. Grave illness, too, may often
attract extremely expensive medical care which is not usually covered
by insurance – for example, serious motorcycle accidents involving
adolescents, or serious cardiac and kidney cases which require
transplant surgery. Expensive urgent treatment cannot be left, in any
civilized society, exclusively as a privilege of the rich, or the heavily
insured, or some other favoured category. So while a prudent person
may take out insurance – and usually does when going on a package
holiday overseas – as a protection against the unexpected serious
illness, most people seem not to do this except when required to do so.
But, of course, all of us in Britain have lived for years in a country
where medical care has been 'free', and we are therefore usually
unwilling to pay for it ourselves except as taxpayers.

It would also be foolish to charge for general practitioners' services
while hospitals are free; to charge for one and not the other would drive
even more patients in through the doors of the hospital. This is what
happened in the days of the old infirmaries, when poor patients from
the locality tended to gravitate to the out-patient departments of
famous hospitals in order to avoid having to pay for the doctor and in
order to get better care. As has been argued, change may be making
the great expensive hospital, for so long the showpiece of medical care,
less dominant, and the battle for health may be being fought more on
the front line by primary health-care teams and GPs. The solution
suggested below is that each course of treatment, following a diagnosis,
should be paid for by a standard sum, drawn from taxation, insurance
and patient expenditure, and that the sum should be allocated to the
hospital or the primary-care team providing the treatment. What is
certain is that the existing system cannot cope with the costs of all the
new treatment that is now becoming available. But the system must be
considered as a whole and not piecemeal, nor biased one way or the
other by the charging system. Care by general practitioners must not be
financed separately from care in hospitals.

The system must also include routine antenatal and postnatal care, the immunization of infants and schoolchildren, the screening of adults for cancer and for high blood pressure and the regular testing of vulnerable groups, all of which are now usually provided by public authorities free in order to encourage the early take-up of care.

Discussions of environmental health and routine testing lead us into preventive medicine. The aim of a health-care system must be to keep people healthy. This goes far wider than immunization. It includes the dissemination of information and the inculcation of healthy habits – not smoking, exercise, good dietary intake, the avoidance of stress and anxiety, all of which have been identified in an earlier chapter as positively causing ill-health. This is not a matter for doctors. It represents a major investment in health by non-medical trades and professions: the food and drink industries, the makers of car safety equipment, the designers of home appliances and the manufacturers of hundreds of goods which are used domestically and in industry. Preventive medicine, clearly, has important consequences for the provision of health care. A health-care planner, whether a government official, a student deciding on a medical career or a businessman deciding where he will place his investment in health-care facilities, has to take a view of the next twenty or thirty years and to decide what the medical needs will be in the future for which provision ought to be made.

The services that have just been alluded to require both state and voluntary action. They do not seem to me to be likely to be taken care of, or financed by, 'market forces'. The idea of 'privatizing' this part of the health budget is unrealistic. The problem is to generate public support for the necessary public action and public expenditure.

At present discussion about the financing of health care lays emphasis on hospitals, drugs and doctors. The indisputable realm for public expenditure is not, however, the Health Service seen in those terms. It is preventive medicine. Should we spend more on hospitals or on health? But – as I shall shortly argue – preventive medicine includes sport, relaxation, a healthy diet. Should these be publicly provided? (The answer is not obvious in the case of active sport, though presumably no one would suggest that all food that is good for us should be free.)

64

First, the need for more thorough provision of preventive and environmental medicine. Not only do the measures taken at present need to be maintained, but they have also to be universalized. (For example, immunization against measles and whooping cough is not yet sufficiently widespread to prevent occasional outbreaks.) There can be no doubt that further immunization and screening procedures will become widely available in the next quarter of a century, which will enable non-infectious diseases to be tackled at source. This will require ever-greater effort in community medicine.

Next comes the need for positive action over environmental health. That is a matter of cleaning up the environment not only in the obvious sense, such as the control of lead pollution to reduce brain damage, but also in the less obvious sense of preventing accidents or illness. For example, the entire population is now motorized, but deaths from traffic accidents are fewer than they were fifty years ago. In 1961, 349,000 people were killed or injured on the roads; in 1980 despite more traffic, the toll had dropped to 328,000. This was the result of crash helmets for motor cyclists, speed limits, pedestrian crossings, traffic lights, seat belts for motorists and greater attention to road safety. Britain now has proportionately fewer road deaths than any other European country.

The same is true of industrial accidents. As the mining and manufacturing industries employ fewer people, so the number of accidents declines; and as the newer industries develop, so the level of safety at work is progressively raised, as in the case of atomic energy or North Sea oil, to say nothing of office work. Only 487 people were killed at work in 1979, less than half the figure for twenty years before. Coalmining accidents fell from 26,100 per 100,000 coalminers in 1971 to 15,200 in 1980, and the number of coalminers fell from 750,000 in 1950 to under 250,000 in 1980. In manufacturing the accident rate per 100,000 workers dropped from 3,500 to 2,900 between 1971 and 1980, and the numbers employed in manufacturing fell by over 1 million.

Many instances can be given of the apparently esoteric forms of preventive medicine which will save lives and reduce suffering. Safety in the home is perhaps one of those most often overlooked. A high proportion of accidents occur at home – falling downstairs, tripping over obstacles, serious cuts, burns and scalds – all of which can, in principle, be avoided. To a considerable extent it is a matter of better design for housing and equipment and of higher safety standards of manufacture. In 1979, 6,545 people died in accidents at home, 3,600 of whom were over the age of 65. A great deal could be done to reduce these figures.

Third, much preventive medicine is concerned with the promotion of positive health. This means encouraging sport and exercise; discouraging alcohol abuse, smoking, the eating of animal fats and sugar; suggesting less stressful living habits, more weight control; and persuading people to eat more fibre in their diet and less salt. Such an improved lifestyle would enormously reduce heart disease and lung cancer, constipation, diverticular disease, overweight and obesity, and would cut down allergies, gall bladder diseases, strokes and tooth decay. The potential saving in money terms would be enormous – a figure of £1,000 million pounds a year has been suggested. British teeth, for example, are a disgrace. Children eat too much, and of the wrong foods. We could, it has been said, save £16 million a year on dentistry alone if we ate less refined sugar and so reduced tooth decay.

Looking ahead, over the next thirty years or so, therefore, by far the most important field for development is environmental and preventive medicine. Some of this will have to be provided by public authorities – pollution control, for example – or enforced by law, as in the case of road safety. Much of it will require propaganda campaigns to counteract tobacco and drink advertising and to promote positive health. But much of what needs to be done could be placed in the hands of private enterprise – fitness and sport, for example. It is ridiculous that municipal swimming pools are not open when adults want to use them and are frequently unattractive; the leisure and recreation industry should step in here, since the public sector seems so dilatory. Thus much of the development of health care over the next thirty years will be in areas which are not now defined as health-care expenditure.

Administering a health-care system that lays emphasis on preventive medicine will be especially complex, since there is a vested interest among the professions caring for the sick but a far less powerful lobby for the positive development of health. The tobacco industry, for example, is powerful; the anti-smoking campaign is comparatively weak. The health professions will turn (one hopes) more and more to prevention as well as cure.

The next area of health care that will develop will again not be what might be called health care proper. This is geriatric medicine. The point has already been made that people are not living longer in general but more are surviving into advanced old age and their numbers are growing as a proportion of the population, as was shown above. By the year 2000, much the same proportion of the population will be over 60 but there will be 500,000 more people over 75.

Older people are vulnerable to common illnesses – coughs and colds, bronchitis, heart trouble and cancer – and will benefit from the cure and relief of such conditions that research and development and the second pharmacological revolution will bring about. But older people have specific problems that can be ameliorated. One is poor sight and deafness, for which increasingly sophisticated aids will be available as a result of micro-electronic development. Another (not due entirely to poor sight and deafness) is vulnerability to accidents. Attention to design and safety, particularly in the home, will reduce accidents, especially among children and the elderly. A third problem may be solved as a consequence of economic and technological development: better telecommunications may help to reduce loneliness and isolation. These are possibilities that need study. But two other problems may well be near solution. Senile confusion and dementia are partly the results of other (often undiagnosed) conditions; depression, for example, is often a cause of confusion. Once the primary condition has been treated, the apparent confusion is reduced. There are now also specific pharmaceuticals which will treat directly the process of senile confusion and possibly dementia itself. Thus one of the curses of old age, a sort of gentle and occasionally violent pottiness, is amenable to treatment. So, too, is the other curse, incontinence. Most people are aware that colostomies can be treated by means of a bag, but the use of catheters, which now often lead to infection, will be much improved, as will other techniques. The distress of incontinence may well be substantially alleviated as a result.

Thus looking after the elderly will be not only a challenge but also an opportunity, having little to do with 'medicine' itself, as conventionally understood, but a great deal to do with the social arrangements made to cope with their problems. American studies by the Institute of Poverty Research shows that elderly people earn 90 per cent of the income of the middle-aged, the result of superannuation. As their purchasing power rises, as one of the consequences of the recent swing to a high proportion of the elderly in the population, so will the production of goods and services designed specifically to meet their needs. Social policy should be directed both to enhancing their purchasing power by adequate pension arrangements and (where necessary) to supplementing it. Sheltered housing, for example, makes an important contribution to the de-medicalizing of the problems of old age. People can arrange for sheltered housing for themselves, as well as waiting for it to be provided.

Among the declining proportion of the population which children and the young will represent the medical problems are well known and, for the most part, well addressed. The Court Report on child health recommended that in each group practice one doctor should specialize in paediatrics and that more attention should be paid to early diagnosis and treatment of children's illnesses. It will be appreciated that the major revolution in child health has already taken place with the substantial elimination of many infections. There are several areas which need (and will receive) attention. The first is to ensure that antenatal and postnatal care is of the highest quality. The differences in infant mortality and morbidity rates for different social groups are sufficiently startling to indicate what needs to be done to improve matters. The United Kingdom has about average perinatal and infant mortality rates for advanced countries and almost the lowest maternal mortality rate. But the mortality rate among babies born to the wives of professional-class fathers is half (9 per 1,000 births) that of wives of unskilled workers (16 per 1,000 births). (Chronic illness is reported by 11 per cent of families from professional groups and 28 per cent of those from unskilled worker groups.) After that, the development of preventive medicine – immunization and regular checks on physical condition – will lead to the introduction of good nutritional habits, which will help to ensure the reduction of, for example, subsequent heart disease and dental illness.

All these points are related to preventive medicine in the conventional sense, but the bulk of serious childhood illness is psychological and social. It is the consequence of broken homes, maternal deprivation and a host of other family, personal and social problems. The handling of these matters, in so far as they are handled at all, is the responsibility of parents, teachers and social workers. The evidence suggests that the success rate of social work is negligible, probably because the problems are ill-defined and the procedures rudimentary in the extreme. Nevertheless, although the problems are not medical, in the sense that they are not strictly the province of a doctor, they shade into the medical field when depression, anxiety and other clinical symptoms become sufficiently serious to require medical treatment. The demand for care is there: 11 per cent of children are members of one-parent families, and presumably many of them suffer from such problems. Whether the demand can be adequately met is another question.

In the vexed area of psychology and psychiatry remarkable changes have taken place already or are foreseen. Many of the questions – as so often in the early stages of the development of effective therapy – are made answerable by being redefined. Nowhere does the shifting boundary between unhappiness, unacceptable behaviour, illness, sadness, grief less easily lend itself to exact formulation, unless the extremes are taken as the starting point for a definition. The clearly mad and the clearly sane define themselves well enough. But by far the greater part of psychiatric treatment and most psychotropic drugs are prescribed for people who, correctly, regard themselves as 'normal' but who have a temporary problem, often arising from stress, insomnia, anxiety, depression, and for whom only temporary relief is sought. In most cases time will be the healer, but drugs (like alcohol) can provide relief from the pain and distress. Such medicines are being continually developed and improved. The breakthrough of the second pharmacological revolution will be relief for sufferers from the serious psychiatric conditions – schizophrenia, autism, manic depression – which have a physiological basis whose mechanisms are only now being understood. A 'cure' is not beyond the bounds of possibility, nor is a more substantial alleviation of the problems of those who are distressed, depressed, anxious or grief-stricken.

Thus in the case of psychiatric illness the probability is that the trend towards less institutional care, observed since the first pharmacological revolution, will accelerate. It will require more, not less, community care and and greater expenditure on necessary medication. But the total outlay will certainly diminish.

The incidence of the other major physical illnesses will ultimately also fall as the mechanisms of disease are more fully understood. Already, for example, large numbers of cases of heart disease and cancer are treatable, and it is known that a substantial number are preventable. They are preventable, however, by changes in lifestyle rather than by a process of immunization. The search for 'immunization-type' cures is illusory, given the present state of knowledge, but the rate of attack can be reduced, and effective treatment after onset is common even now and will become increasingly so as knowledge extends and techniques improve. Once more, much treatment is likely to be pharmacologically based.

It can be forecast with an equal degree of certainty that further research will lead to the alleviation of many conditions which until now have been effectively untreatable or treatable only at high cost, such as chronic kidney failure, which necessitates dialysis and kidney transplants for only a few thousand people. The scope of therapy, therefore, will be broadened and deepened, and the number of diseases which can now be only nursed sympathetically will diminish, while the number of diseases that can be actively treated will increase.

What will be the effects of these developments, all of them foreseen and, in most cases, already under way? The answer to this question – which is twofold, since it concerns both cost and organization – is considered in the next two chapters.

7

Rising Expenditure

In *Health Care and its Costs* the Government estimated in 1983 that the effect of technological innovation was to raise costs by 0.5 per cent a year. What does the word 'cost' mean in this context? We have noted that the cost of each individual treatment may diminish as it becomes routine, but in consequence there are many more treatable cases. Hip replacement, for example, was once tricky and rare: it is now common. The same is true of heart artery by-pass surgery, of many courses of drug therapy and of general surgery, a field in which medical technology has made previously experimental treatments available to a large number of people. The cost of each treatment decreases, but the benefits are far more widespread. This is indeed a source of rising expenditure in health care, but it is a little ambiguous to call such an increase in expenditure an 'increase in costs'.

Take a simple analogy. In 1945 there was no expenditure on microcircuitry. There is now an immense complex of industries throughout the world serving a vast consumer market. This is undoubtedly 'increased expenditure'. It is not a sensible use of language to call it 'increased costs'. In other words, a demand for a series of new products and services has been created by the market, and as the market has expanded the technology has advanced and the unit costs of each individual item has fallen. There is a simple pattern: high development costs of a new product, high unit costs initially and falling unit costs as output expands. Medical innovation follows exactly the same pattern, if only because it rests primarily upon the pharmaceutical industry, which is an industry that is concerned primarily with innovation.

The difference between electronics on the one hand and high-technology medicine on the other is that the first is sold in the market

71

and the second is provided largely by the public sector. The electronics industry is thus seen as adding to economic output, while high-technology health care is seen as adding to public expenses and as a drain upon the economic output to which the electronics industry is contributing. Clearly, there is a conceptual error in this way of looking at things: health care, after all, is not a 'drain on output' if people need it and are prepared to pay for it. But there is certainly a difference of view between those who are attempting to limit public expenditure and those who want better health care. An attempt to discuss fully the complex questions of how health care is paid for and how it might be paid for will be made later, but the issue is raised here in order to make it absolutely clear that rising expenditure is not synonymous with rising cost: moreover, rising expenditure is desirable if it gives people what they want – more comfortable, happier lives with less ill-health.

It would be true to say, however, that the development of high-technology medicine has led to increases in outlays, whether these be called an 'increase in costs' or 'expenditure' or whatever; furthermore, it is virtually certain that high-technology medicine will accelerate for two main reasons. First, the pharmacological revolution which we are now witnessing is based on breakthroughs in basic science, especially biochemistry and biophysics, and it is from this scientific development, which is itself still accelerating, that the fuller understanding of immunology, of the treatment of viruses, of cancer and of genetic malfunctioning will come. These breakthroughs will lead to pharmaceutical and other innovations, which will in turn make possible new medical and surgical procedures. Second, the main strand of high technology is the application of contemporary developments in micro-circuitry and new materials to medical matters ranging from the use of the computer in diagnosis and in epidemiology, to the use of tiny catheters in surgery. These various developments – and there are many of them – enormously increase the likelihood of the effective treatment of illnesses. The demand for treatment is certain to grow, therefore, even were the incidence of illness to diminish, since it is the concept of the *treatable illness* that determines demand rather than the actual amount of illness – which (according to the definition of

72

the World Health Organization in chapter 1, for example) is virtually limitless.

One major consequence of technological and scientific advance, then, is to emphasize the locations in which high technology can be utilized. This may seem a self-evident truth, but it is not. For example, the linking of testing procedures – X-rays, laboratories for analysing blood and tissue, electrocardiograms – in a hospital suggests the importance of getting patients to a hospital. But it is possible to decentralize many of these procedures, especially as the machinery is miniaturized and becomes cheaper and more standard. Some will soon even be housed in mobile vans, as chest X-ray units and blood-donor clinics already are.

High-technology medicine has already had far-reaching effects on the pattern of medical care, but so far only the early stages of a fundamental revolution have been seen. We have noticed the change in the number of people wanting specialist surgery, such as hip replacements, and we have seen that this has so far meant that more people have entered hospitals to have such surgery carried out. There are further changes to be made, however. The technological revolution which has so far prompted initial changes in patterns of medical care has led to talk of an 'explosion' in costs. These violent metaphors of revolution and explosion suggest the degree and pace of change which is being analysed, but they do not take sufficiently into account the nature of the change.

It is possible to peer into the future and to discern several new trends in health care. Geriatrics and chronic cases of severe mental illness and mental handicap will probably be moved into community houses or will be given some degree of non-institutional care. This will not be cheaper than hospital care, but its costs will fall on different social agencies, for whom it will present severe financial and organizational problems, especially as the number of people aged 80 and over increases fairly rapidly, for it is that group that needs more care.

More and more people will require diagnosis and treatment in acute hospitals because the speed of medical advance is such that what now seem very innovative techniques – whole-body scanning, for example – will become widely available. On the other hand, the length of time

73

each patient spends as an 'in'-patient will fall, since treatment will be more efficacious and speedier, and the emphasis in medical care now is on shortening hospital stays. The need to be near a hospital is declining, as more of the population is motorized and short-stay patients need fewer visitors, so small local hospitals will continue to be closed, while larger hospitals, with batteries of diagnostic equipment, will develop.

But the effect of these changes is certain to make the general practitioner or (the 'primary health-care team', as we ought to call the GP and his or her colleagues) far more of a 'treater' of serious illness than he is at present. Thus the role of the GP as the first stop on the road to the hospital will decline as the battery of treatment and diagnostic aids that he has immediately available will increase: fewer people will need to enter hospital.

What is at issue is growing public demand for modern high tech-nology, which in the private sector has been shown to be very high. From the introduction of television it took less than twenty years for its spread to reach saturation point, that is, the stage at which almost every family had at least one television set. The dispersal of transistor radios was quicker, that of motor cars slower, but clearly it is the same phenomenon that has been observed in each case. There is every reason to suppose that the same will be true of medical care.

But medical care is mediated through the professions, especially the medical profession, so that public demand is not relayed directly to the retailer. This is so whether the medical care is publicly or privately provided. The medical profession therefore exercises a powerful influence on the progress of the technology and on its acceptability and availability to the public.

Because the most powerful doctors have been connected with university teaching hospitals, it is these hospitals that have tended to become the focus of high-technology medicine. Now, however, there is an equally strong case for locating much of the equipment with the primary medical-care team in local health centres or in institutions or laboratories which are independent both of hospitals and of local doctors.

High-technology medicine does not have to mean ever more expensive and bigger hospitals whose activity is centred on the out-patient wing and fewer hospitals devoted to the concept of the in-patient, the patient who is mainly in bed. In terms of medical consultation and procedure at the moment, modern hospitals are mostly for out-patients, that is, those who visit to keep a specific appointment; but this does not have to continue to be so. Obviously, acute cases, heart surgery, cancer operations and the like will continue to be treated in hospitals, but the pattern of general hospital use is changing. In recent years one in eight of the population has been in hospital, and everybody has had one out-patient consultation – that is, of course, an average that includes many who do not go near a hospital and some who are frequent visitors. But, again on average, everybody goes to a general practitioner every seven or eight weeks. This chain of reasoning suggests not that high-technology medicine will inevitably require more outlays, as is commonly supposed, but that the pattern of provision in the future may be even less hospital-dominated than it is now.

Incidentally, it is worth observing at this juncture that there are two deeply rooted attitudes which encourage people unwittingly to opt for the status quo in medicine. The first is the conviction that medicine is identified with emergency, with life-saving, with surgery – which is far from the truth. This idea is, of course, fostered by the fact that hospital is the place to which urgent and serious cases are taken, that one in twenty of the cases ferried by ambulance are emergencies and that in a crisis 'send for the doctor' is a popular cry. Indeed, it is notable that anything which is even remotely related to doctors, hospitals, drugs or medication carries with it the connotation of urgency, of seriouness, which has profound psychological force. This leads to the second attitude, which is that the suggestion that anything medical has a place in ordinary commercial life is likely to arouse responses that are extremely strong. It is assumed, for example, that to look for profit in the marketing of drugs is to 'play' with life, to 'profit from sickness'; in the medical field, it is argued, no decision should have anything to do with something as frivolous as consumer choice. And to pay attention to a demand for privacy, good food, convenience in hospital provision is regarded as seeking to provide 'frills', as detracting from the serious nature of illness. To take a significant example, the proposition that the doctor's time is more valuable than the patient's is sometimes, but not always, true: in each individual case the comparison is a matter of fact. But public policy is based on public attitudes, and public attitudes are dominated by the idea of the doctor as the life-saver, therefore his or her time is believed to be infinitely more precious than that of any patient.

Thus the present role of the hospital as the pivot of health care rests upon a number of considerations: hospitals are where the high technology is, where ambulances race to, where acute surgery is carried out, where lives are saved, where the latest advanced surgery techniques are pioneered and where doctors function most efficiently. Not least of these considerations is the power and prestige of the consultants, though which is cause and which is effect is not clear. A consultant decides what treatments are acceptable and available and what the patient may have. He is at the top of the tree, and so he makes his treetop the tallest in the forest, and as he works in a hospital, the hospital shares in his eminence. On the other hand, as we have seen, the tree is tall because it deals with life-saving procedures and difficult cases and uses a great deal of expensive equipment.

Will hospitals continue to be the pivot of health care as medical technology accelerates, or will this role pass to the general practitioner?

The general practitioner has shifted from being the wise (but, if the truth be told, ineffective) counsellor and friend of his patients to being the dispenser of life-saving and condition-relieving drugs. His room is now the centre of medical advice for the area, for it is he who makes the initial diagnosis of what is wrong and what can be done; he tells his patients what facilities are available; and it is he who refers them for specialist advice to the hospital if need be. He also provides routine health checks, vaccines and immunization injections. He will often himself treat a number of illnesses which can be cured, or at least stabilized, by the use of drugs without referring them to further specialists, but at other times he will send patients to hospital and will then carry on with the therapies which have been initiated by the specialist in the hospital. Coronary care is a good example, for the great majority of cardiac patients are sent home after a brief spell in hospital to be treated by their GPs.

The GP is also the central figure for the primary health teams, for nurses working in the community, for health visitors, for school doctors, for physiotherapists and that growing number of people who help the elderly in the community, for those recovering from accidents, for patients with osteo-arthritis and for those whose pain can be alleviated by drugs but who require encouragement, help, counselling, specialist exercises and individual home visits.

Unfortunately, the doctor's training is at present too hospital-centred and lays too little emphasis on the idea of the doctor as part of a team in the community (not in the generalized, pejorative, social-worker sense of that much abused term but as one specialist among many who can contribute and use information from diverse sources to enable a patient to choose the most efficacious, acceptable and cheapest way to health). The idea that a patient may actively look after himself or herself, weigh up medical options and make a choice is fundamentally at odds with the paternalism of the doctor who has been trained to dispense advice and treatment to ignorant patients and of the welfare state which 'looks after' you on its own terms. In a free society, where more and more people are well informed (or even partially informed), people need to be persuaded to alter their lifestyles to prevent illness and to seek and evaluate medical advice drawn from modern basic science. Doctors must be trained to inform their patients, to educate them and to help them restyle their lives, even if it means increasing the length of medical training so that it becomes more expensive.

The GP will also have to receive greater training in psychiatric counselling, for he will be dealing with many more cases in the local community. While severe mental conditions and moderate anxiety and depression will be treated pharmaceutically, the listening and counselling side of general practice will become more and more important. Medicine today has a number of social roles which are growing in variety and significance. General practitioners will find themselves involved increasingly with that grey area where medical fields shade off into

77

non-medical areas for example, marriage guidance and family planning. Family planning has only comparatively recently become part of the customary range of services provided by general practitioners, and fertility, of course, has been greatly affected by the Pill. As contraception develops, so the role of the primary health-care team in this field will also extend.

General practitioners are already extremely busy: they are going to be even busier with the growth of emphasis and expenditure on primary health care. And while GPs are an alternative to high-technology hospital provision, they are themselves applying high technology but in a different way: they are not therefore a cheap alternative.

The training of the doctor and his colleagues is long and expensive, and so too is the cost of paying them and keeping them in satisfactory premises. Since their main initial task is diagnosis, the equipment they require is also expensive, ranging from laboratory to X-ray equipment. This can be shared among group practices or placed in a health centre, but it still has to be paid for. There is the cost of maintaining records. In addition, there are all the routine health checks, including programmes of immunization and vaccination, none of which is cheap, though most of them are commonplace. All this routine and very important work buttresses courses of pharmaceutical treatment, which are not cheap either.

In this chapter I have explained how high-technology medicine has changed not merely the pattern but the very nature of health care and hence of health costs. More illnesses are treatable and more people now demand operations which will make their lives happier and healthier. This means that more money has to be spent on medical care in all its aspects, both in hospitals and in the community. Costs for individual operations have come down as they have become less rare and as more people have demanded them, but just because they are more popular, the number accomplished has risen, which has increased expenditure on them as a whole. Some costs are being saved as more and more sickness is being treated in the community by primary health teams using pharmaceutical and other techniques which were hitherto available only in hospitals: other costs have shifted from hospitals to the general practitioner. But just as it looked as if overall medical costs could be scaled down by decreasing the size and number of hospitals, so the front line community-care system expanded to cover a wider field. All the time the demand for more health care has grown, and the kinds of problem which come within the general practitioner's brief have increased: the entire field of what is considered medicine is expanding its frontiers. Where the money goes, what it is spent on and how it is spent has changed; at the same time the range of facilities which health care expenditure covers has expanded.

8

Organizing Health Care

We have seen that medical care is undergoing a profound change. Not only has there been a series of advances in research, in techniques, in drugs, but also priorities are being reconsidered because both medicine itself and perceptions of what medicine can do are changing, as are people's expectations.

The problems which have to be tackled are, first, how to organize health care – by this I mean who is to provide the services to ensure that there are enough hospitals and doctors and drugs – and, second, who is to pay for the care? At present in Britain the state has inherited a set of buildings and a body of staff to which, over the years, it has added. Our analysis suggests that the total amount of resources devoted to health care, in its broadest sense, will increase as new technology makes it possible to treat successfully more and more conditions. It is by no means obvious that the state is the only, or the best, provider and organizer of services. It is suggested, here and in succeeding chapters, that the wider definition of health care and the rising wealth of the community demand a diversity of provision.

Inescapably, it seems to me, in a service that is developing and changing so rapidly this means that there will not be uniformity of provision; it takes time for one technique to emerge as clearly the best, and new techniques are continually being developed at different centres of medical research and innovation. Furthermore, much new treatment requires, in its early stages, an arbitrary selection of patients. Any system of choosing patients for treatment will be arbitrary if resources are limited as by definition they are particularly for new and expensive forms of medical care.

Within the limits of the resources available, decisions about medical care are always ultimately in the hands of professionals, especially doctors, but of course the doctors are influenced by patient demand, which can take different forms, pleading, bullying or payment, the last being perhaps the most persuasive. Since all treatment is to some degree a gamble, different doctors will have different criteria for judging what treatment is required by the same patient. But some treatments are so expensive that they have to be rationed not only by the doctors but also by the 'providing authority', the hospital, or the national authority, or the insurance company. Again, it must be emphasized that choosing patients for, say, heart transplants is in the end an arbitrary matter, however apparently sophisticated the criterion applied. (In the present state of public opinion, however, it is not permissible to take into account the wealth of the patient, though this ignores the fact that the rich patient can go to another country if he or she is refused treatment here.)

The 'organization of health care' raises issues such as who decides what hospitals should be opened or closed, what their range of specialities should be and what primary care and other health facilities should be available. These matters may be decided nationally, as in Britain, where the central government delegates its powers to regional bodies, or they may be resolved by a combination of local government and private enterprise, as in most other countries.

That question of organization is, of course, closely related to how health care is paid for – out of taxes, through insurance (which can be compulsory or voluntary), directly by individuals and families or by charities. One of the arguments of this book is that the costs of health care are bound to rise as the scope and efficacy of health care increase, and that it is desirable (and probably inevitable) that health care will be provided by a growing variety of arrangements. It is highly likely (and desirable) that this will entail a diversity of sources of funding. Later I shall consider who will pay for health care and how. At this stage I wish to outline how health care expenditure will increase.

In the first place, though the bulk of health-care expenditure goes on hospital provision, we have seen that the main reason for this bias is not high-technology medicine as it is conventionally understood – heart transplants, for example – but rather the fact that serious acute care is almost inescapably a matter for hospitals. Also the possibility of successfully treating common diseases, like cardiac illness and cancer, is increasing daily, so it follows, that the number of patients who can be successfully treated will rise and will therefore increase the hospital load. Largely as a result of the second pharmacological revolution, the scope of effective primary medical care is also continuously growing. Courses of pills or injections can now cure most bacterial infections, and an increasing range of drugs is available for the treatment of other illnesses. Thus the scope of successful medical treatment is continually extending, and extending particularly rapidly in the primary-care field. To this must be added the other primary health-care tasks – looking after chronic patients, helping the elderly, caring for the anxious and depressed – as well as the short-term rehabilitation of people who have had relatively minor accidents (a broken arm or leg, for instance).

As advances take place in medical practice and in the understanding of social problems, so the possibility of alleviating pain and distress will constantly increase. Two examples may suffice to illustrate this point. The first is geriatric care, and the second is relatively mild psychiatric illness.

As people grow older, so they begin to run down physically and to suffer the loss both of loved ones and of income. Their needs change as their circumstances change. Among those who survive to 65 a great deal of distress is caused by social isolation (they may have moved to the seaside away from friends and family), by confusion and dementia, by incontinence and by increasing physical feebleness. Social support, such as visitors and old people's clubs, homehelps and meals-on-wheels, and appropriately adapted housing can mitigate much of the distress and isolation. Activity and exercise can stave off feebleness. Above all, through careful diagnosis and treatment of ordinary illnesses much apparent confusion and dementia can be avoided. (It is increasingly recognized, for example, that elderly people need different food and liquid intakes than other age groups.) Increasingly, too, simple technological devices will reduce the problem of incontinence, as we have noted.

Thus, for a fortunate elderly person – fortunate, that is, in the level and kind of social and medical provision available to him or her – the difficulties of old age can already be significantly reduced, and many of these difficulties will in turn be further reduced as geriatric services improve. With a large number of elderly people in the population, the significance of their medical and social needs is increasing. In order, therefore, to take advantage of what is now possible, much additional expenditure will be required. The question is: how is this expenditure to be met?

Inevitably, it will be met in part by the state, since some elderly people will have neither the means to pay for care nor relatives to organize it. But, increasingly, elderly people have adequate insurance cover and income. And, in a society where a growing proportion of people own their own homes and have capital assets, many elderly people have capital. So it is not unreasonable that a proportion of their medical needs – which shade into social needs – should be paid for by elderly people themselves. It is highly likely that there will be more and more private provision of health care for the elderly in response to their own capacity for expenditure.

A second example will reinforce the point that successful medical and social developments entail additional expenditure. It concerns mental health. Apart from the more caring and concerned attitude towards anxiety and depression and towards the social problems associated with them, such as family breakdown, there is an increasing volume of pharmaceutical preparations which relieve anxiety, lift depression and reduce insomnia. Despite the prevalence of views that a society in which so many people take sedatives, narcotics and hypnotics is itself unhealthy, and despite the widespread evidence of lax prescribing on the basis of inadequate medical and social counselling, there can be little doubt that much misery has been alleviated by these preparations. Furthermore, new biochemical research indicates clearly that there is a physical basis at least for some, if not all, of the conditions that have been treated so far by valium and other preparations, and that a major series of new drugs will become available which will deal directly with the cause of the problems, rather than merely alleviating the symptoms. Desite all the dangers of side-effects, of 'masking' problems that are better resolved by psycho-therapy and of other difficulties, there can be little doubt that the new drugs will be widely used, that they will mitigate misery and unhappiness and that they will also significantly reduce short-term stays in acute psychiatric wards and other 'asylums' (in the proper sense of the word). There is also a genuine prospect that addiction to alcohol may well be controlled by drug therapy, since alcoholism now seems in part to have a physical cause. In a whole range of social and psychiatric illness, therefore, a real prospect is opening up of breakthroughs based on scientific knowledge which will allow some of the most distressing symptoms to be controlled or even eliminated. Leaving on one side, for the moment, the ethical and other problems associated with the treatment of a range of illnesses which have traditionally been associated with unhappiness rather than with physical affliction, there are now abundant indications that these illnesses, however defined, will shortly be actively treatable.

The explosion in demand for psychotropic drugs has given an indication of the likely demand for the new therapies. They will be available, like antibiotics, from the primary-care team – specifically, the general practitioner. Their impact will be to raise the costs and scale of primary care and to reduce the costs of institutional and hospital care. This poses the question of how care is to be organized, since it is split at present between social agencies of all kinds, the medical team, the hospitals' acute and psychiatric wards, hostels for alcoholics, vagrants and others, the conditions of many of whose patients and inmates will become treatable in the clinical medical sense. It also raises the question of how this great growth in primary-care expenditure is to be met. The expenditure will to some degree, obviously, be provided by the state. But, again, as in the case of the elderly, people requiring care of the kind just alluded to may well be keen to make their own provision. There is, indeed, a strong argument for encouraging this, quite apart from the need to restrict public expenditure: dependence on the free issue of medicines is in itself a reflection of the 'dependence' of the patient (on drugs or alcohol) which the treatment is designed to overcome. To earn enough to pay for treatment may well itself be therapeutic, as most psychoanalysts have long urged.

So in two instances, old age and conditions associated with depression and anxiety, advances in medical knowledge will in themselves add to the demand for medical care while at the same time offering the prospect of alleviating distress – though not necessarily contributing to the nation's economic strength, since the elderly are by and large consumers and not earners, spenders and not savers, and little psychiatric illness results in days off work.

These examples have been included to round out the perspective yielded by the spectacular advances that are on the threshold for cardio-vascular disease, cancer and the major psychiatric illnesses, especially schizophrenia. In all of these instances there will be the possibility of the successful treatment of conditions which have hitherto been treated generally on a 'care and maintenance' basis. In the case of auto-immune diseases, like early-onset diabetes, multiple sclerosis and possibly rheumatoid arthritis, to cite the examples of Professor George Teeling-Smith,* there is the possibility, too, of active and successful treatment.

In the longer run, of course, in many cases there will be some simple, easy and, above all, cheap treatment – probably a series of injections or pills – which will reduce medical costs and will provide at least relief from suffering ranging from the mild to the severe. But it is far too simple to suppose that the medical developments now under way or realistically foreseeable will reduce expenditure on medical care, if only for the simple reason that active medical care will become possible for a whole range of patients who at the moment are not successfully treatable. Nor is it enough to say that active medical treatment will switch from the hospital to the primary health-care team. In the case of bacterial infections that has indeed happened, but much treatment – for example, of cancer – is likely to remain for some years generally a hospital matter. In the longer run, of course, diagnosis and treatment will become so routinized that it will be handed out to the primary health-care team, but the evidence suggests that over the next twenty years there will be growth in both sectors. Thus growth in primary care cannot take place at the expense of hospital care without leaving untreated a whole range of cases which it would in practise prove impossible to neglect or leave untreated. Nobody with cancer wants to go on a waiting list.

*The Second Pharmacological Revolution, ed. Nicholas Wells (the Office of Health Economics publication), 1983.

In short, expenditure on medical care will rise. Some of the increase will be an added burden on public expenditure, but some can be met by private sources – sport, recreation and other preventive medicine, equipment to promote comfort and ease – and some can be funded by insurance. A careful analysis needs to be made of future expenditure and how it can be met; a preliminary set of suggestions is offered in chapter 11.

As the future costs of health care are going to be so huge, some people think that it would be a good idea to establish priorities, to choose between expensive, highly technical medical research and that needed by the majority of patients. Such people appear to imagine that it is a simple matter of choosing between, say, spending less on heart transplants or bone-marrow matching and more on geriatrics, that you can switch medical breakthroughs by diverting money. But this is to misunderstand the whole nature of medical research.

Medical research in Britain is partly funded by the Medical Research Council – and several of the other Research Councils as well, especially as far as basic science is concerned – partly by the universities and, above all, by the pharmaceutical industry. Wherever medical research is actively conducted, the clinical costs are bound to be above-average. It is important, therefore, not to lose sight of the need for centres of excellence. It is also important that the pharmaceutical industry should not be so hemmed in by controls that no advances at all are possible. It has already been shown that this would be a false economy, since medical development costs can lead to cheaper and more effective drug therapies, which people want and are prepared to pay for and which will (ultimately) reduce the cost of treatment per patient in the case of a number of prevalent diseases. However, as has been explained, to look forward to a fall in health-care expenditure as a result of technical progress and innovation is to misunderstand the nature of the question at issue, as the number of *treatable* cases will rise.

The matter is simple. Basic scientific research is undertaken mainly by the Research Councils and the universities. Technical innovation is undertaken by firms, especially pharmaceutical firms, and by the medical and paramedical professions. To attempt to control such development by restrictive controls is bound to limit it, whether the controls are designed to promote 'safety' (by requiring more and more complex testing procedures, for example), are 'restrictive' (in delimiting different markets in Europe) or aim to 'control recurrent expenditure' (to cut costs). There is a balance to be struck, and it is at present being struck in a way that is not favourable to technical progress. The result could be serious, not only for health care but also for the valuable British export trade in pharmaceuticals.

One of the most fundamental facts about science is serendipity, the faculty of making lucky and unexpected finds by chance when one is not actually looking for them. Such accidental discoveries are more likely to be made if a great deal of research is being carried out over a wide field than if research is invested directly in the discovery of a successful therapy for a specific illness. Moreover, discoveries in one field can be applied in another, often with even greater significance. Through such means new uses are often found for old drugs or old medical techniques, or research methods used in one field are applied with startling success in another. For example, those sent to teach gunners how to fire more accurately in the Second World War needed to know how the eye tracked a moving target and sent this information to the muscles. After the war this newly acquired information was applied with remarkable success to the investigation of control systems, cybernetics and neurophysiology.

Scientists have been conducting research into the causes of cancer for many years now. A vast amount of money, equipment, high technology and hundreds of man hours have been expended, and there have been some 'breakthroughs', although this is a misleading word for what have really been slow, steady and remorseless advances on a broad front. Many leads are followed up which come to dead ends, yet they have to be taken to their conclusions in case they turn out to be crucial. Sometimes researchers in entirely different fields make discoveries which are helpful to the cancer workers – odd leads turn up in the work of those who are studying biophysics, embryology, genetics, cell structure – and slowly these different discoveries are put together to extend our knowledge of the disease. Leukaemia in children is controllable to a certain extent now; other cancers are better understood; and the nature of the organisms involved is clearer. But it is laborious work which cannot be hurried. Even when enough is known to produce a useful drug to alleviate or 'cure' cancer, pharmaceutical firms may have to spend £50 million or more on research and development to make the drug on a large scale.

New surgical procedures are often inescapably expensive while the initial techniques are under development, and the same is true of radiotherapy, body scanners and all the other developments which hit the headlines. Then there is a long pause while the new discovery is adapted and routinized. Slowly it percolates down to regular use, but the gap between breakthrough and routine is long and costly.

The wrong priorities can be chosen through a misunderstanding of the problems. What does it mean in practice, for instance, if priority is given to geriatric care? A lick of paint? A few extra nurses in a geriatric ward? That is what usually happens. But, as has already been argued, the real breakthrough in geriatric care will consist of drugs to alleviate confusion and dementia and the treatment and diagnosis of a whole series of diseases, some of them not serious in themselves but cumulatively incapacitating, and the development of techniques to cope with incontinence. Much of this work is now high technology, and solutions may be found as a result of serendipity in other fields. The issue goes far beyond the development of a new, socially conscious set of priorities which puts the needs of the elderly before heart transplants. Heart transplants will probably always be rare and expensive, but the research associated with organ transplants is in itself of great significance and may be of help to the elderly in unexpected ways.

The free-ranging scientific mind, operating throughout the West to develop the modern biological sciences, is certain to make major breakthroughs, both by chance and on purpose. All the evidence suggests that international pharmaceutical companies will market fresh products which will astonish even those who are accustomed to miracle drugs. This will happen despite the increasing expense of tests and procedures imposed by public bodies for safety's sake and the increasingly strict limits on expenditure on drugs. Equally, a great range of new aids, using modern techniques and materials, will be available for those who are temporarily or permanently handicapped.

The vital matter is to encourage freedom to experiment and innovate and to reward success. Attempts to control priorities and to limit profit, therefore, are certain to be shortsighted and to slow down medical progress.

Serendipity and diversity are the basis, then, of an evolving system of medical care. Such a system requires flexibility if it is to be administered with success, but it will be shown in the next chapter that the United Kingdom's National Health Service is astonishingly rigid and bureaucratic, whereas mainland European systems, described in chapter 10, are more diverse.

9

The National Health Service

The concept of 'free medical care' is not unambiguous. Care of the sick is 'free' at the point of contact between the patient and the doctor in most European countries most of the time, as the next chapter shows. But somebody has to pay the bills. In the United Kingdom it is generally the taxpayer who pays, whereas elsewhere it is an insurance scheme. Since membership of the insurance scheme is usually compulsory, premiums are similar to a tax: they come to much the same thing.

The taxpayer has always paid for much of the medical care of the poor. A case can be made for pointing to the Elizabethan Poor Law as the first evidence of an organized health service in England. By Victorian times the workhouse infirmary had become the basis of a system of general hospitals catering for the indigent to which was allied a system of Poor Law dispensaries offering vestigial general-practitioner care to the very poor. The great teaching hospitals, Bart's, St Thomas's, Guy's and many others, were charitable institutions where the nursing improved after Florence Nightingale's reformation of the profession, and cross-infection was reduced following the introduction of antiseptics. Great asylums were built near towns to segregate the insane, and as medical knowledge grew, so more and more 'specialists' had hospital practices which gave them prestige and enabled them to practise private consultant medical care. They had private patients, many of whom were cared for in private nursing homes or in private wings of the hospitals. Most general practitioners had some beds in local hospitals, where they treated their own patients as well as having access to private nursing homes.

A 'panel' system was introduced by Lloyd George in 1911, which enabled some categories of workers to receive free treatment and medicine from the doctor with whom they were registered. By 1938 this scheme covered much of the male working population but not their wives and children. By that year, too, the modern medical revolution had already begun. The demand for medical care was increasing in consequence, and as the standard of living rose, so people expected better treatment and were prepared to pay for it, either directly or through taxes.

At the end of the First World War the Haldane Committee, set up by the Ministry for Reconstruction in 1918, proposed the formation of a Ministry of Health for England and Wales. This was done, and in 1919 a Consultative Council on Medical and Allied Services was set up under the chairmanship of Lord Dawson of Penn, the royal doctor. The Dawson Report, published in 1920, outlined a plan for a unified and national service providing a basic framework of health-care services. In 1929, when the Poor Law was largely abolished, the local authorities took over the Poor Law hospitals and began to upgrade them. But the Ministry of Health – whose responsibilities then included housing – was not in any sense a Ministry supervising a national system of health care.

The Second World War led to a national hospital service, buttressed by a mixture of panel and private patients served by general practitioners. The Dawson Report had pointed out the need for a single health authority. The pressures were, however, for the medical-care system to be provided by local authorities, although the doctors, for the most part, did not wish to work for the local authorities. It was virtually agreed, therefore, by the end of the war that the hospitals would be nationalized. In the National Health Service Act, 1946, a tripartite system was proposed that offered a compromise, the administrative separation of local authority community services, the hospital service, with private beds, plus independent contracted sectors. The disadvantages of the tripartite structure were obvious. For example, patients with chronic and handicapping conditions requiring both hospital and community-based services suffered from lack of communication between branches. The National Health Service was isolated, too, from other branches of the 'welfare state'.

The hospitals were nationalized and organized under Regional Hospital Boards. The local authorities were given responsibility for environmental health services and domiciliary services (home helps, visiting nurses, ambulances). General practitioners, dentists and chemists (pharmacists) had an independent relationship with the local executive council, composed largely of medical and dental personnel. Hospital doctors and other staff were on a full-time salary, but consultants were permitted private patients and private beds in the nationalized hospitals. General practitioners were paid mainly according to the number of their patients, pharmacists according to the number and costs of prescriptions dispensed and dentists and opticians according to standard charges for courses of treatment and items like spectacles.

The 23,000 or so general practitioners were the cornerstone of the service when it started on 5 July 1948, but rapidly the hospital service became the central arch of the building. The creation of the National Health Service coincided with the great wave of medical innovation described in earlier chapters. There was at first an explosion of costs, as previously unmet demand became evident and as new techniques were widely applied to the treatment of more and more patients with treatable conditions.

The National Health Service rested on two fallacies. The first was that there was a 'backlog' of untreated cases of illness which could be cleared up by adequate care and that thereafter the load of medical work would decline as the nation got healthier. In fact, as this book has shown, progress in medicine means that there are more treatable cases than before. The second fallacy was allied to the first. When the NHS was set up some of the major medical problems appeared to lie in the field of infectious disease, like tuberculosis, although in fact the major drugs for controlling infection, like penicillin, were already in use by 1948, and by the late 1950s most bacterial infection had been conquered. The 'new' enemies of health, cancer and heart disease, had marched on, however. It is by no means clear that the system devised when infection was the major killer was appropriate to the new medical picture.

The National Health Service was extremely popular. Despite its cost to the Exchequer, the idea – and above all the practice – of a service free on demand caught the public fancy: although there were obvious disadvantages (notably, long waiting lists for hospital appointments), it seemed to work to the public advantage.

Its main structure remained unchallenged until the 1960s. The major concern was that the tripartite nature of the NHS, and the way in which power was freely delegated down the line from the centre, led to inadequate follow-through of particular patients. The tripartite formation consisted of hospitals, local authorities (public health and community health services) and executive councils providing general medical services. The system was seen as a hindrance to co-operation and planning. Green Papers were issued for discussion by the Labour Government in 1968 and 1970. In 1971 the Conservative Government issued a consultative document leading to reorganization in 1974. What had happened was that as a result of the tripartite system, the hospitals had come to dominate medical care, though it was widely acknowledged that the bulk of medical treatment should take place outside the hospital, in the community. There was, it seemed, a misallocation of resources.

On 1 April 1974 reorganization took place in England, Scotland and Wales. In 1946 the country had been recovering from the social and economic trauma of war, and a free health service for all symbolized the hopes of post-war Britain for a better future. In 1973 the changes were planned in a system that was taken for granted. Yet both Acts rested on the necessity for compromise between an ideal pattern of health care and constraints imposed by existing resources (both material and human) and the power of the medical profession.

What follows is complex. Its complexity explains its chaos.

The new structure rested on local administrative units, the Area Health Authorities (AHAs), which had statutory responsibility for running the Health Service at local level. They operated (in theory) in parallel with the Districts, but in multi-District areas Districts became almost a fourth tier. AHAs were corporately responsible for health care in geographical areas which were on the whole coterminous with local authority metropolitan districts and non-metropolitan counties, except in the case of London and Merseyside. In all there were ninety English AHAs, of which sixteen were in Greater London.

Scotland was divided into fifteen NHS Area Boards and Wales

into eight. In England the AHAs were grouped together under fourteen Regional Health Authorities (RHAs). Scotland, Wales and Northern Ireland have common Service Agencies, fulfilling (to some degree) the regional health authorities' role. In the 1974 reorganization the Districts were intended to be the smallest units for which substantially the full range of general health and social services could be provided, and also the largest ones within which all types of staff could actively participate in management, through effective representative systems. In 1972 the 'Grey Book' indicated that they would have populations of around 250,000 each, but in fact there was great variation in their sizes, from below 100,000 to about 500,000.

The NHS organization at district level was very complex. It had (a) District Management Teams (DMTs); (b) District Medical Committees (DMCs); (c) Health Care Planning Teams (HCPTs); (d) Community Health Councils (CHCs). Each DMT was composed of a nursing and finance officer, an administrator and a specialist in community medicine (a community physician) and two members of the DMC who represented local consultants and GPs.

District officers managed and co-ordinated many of the operational aspects of NHS services within their localities and helped to formulate policies and plans for the future. DMTs were responsible to the AHA.

Each DMC was composed of ten members drawn from the hospital and community medical staff (including dentists). HCPTs, established by DMTs, conducted detailed local planning for the provision of integrated, individual care for patient groups such as expectant mothers, the elderly, children or various categories of the chronically ill. Each district had several teams.

The CHCs were designed to act as public 'watchdogs' with regard to development of health services. They were not part of the formal management structure but should have had access to NHS plans and premises. They met with AHAs once a year, and published annual reports, to which AHAs were obliged to reply.

The AHAs were the lowest level of statutory authority within the reorganized structure. They employed most of the NHS staff. The organization of an AHA with several districts differed from that which

95

formed one district. In the latter Area Teams of Officers (ATOs), which supported AHA members and held delegated executive powers, played a role similar to that of the DMT. In some circumstances it was known as an Area Management Team (AMT).

AHAs were responsible to RHAs for the running of services as corporate bodies, although individual officers of the ATOs had delegated powers for certain services, for which they were individually accountable. Many members of Authorities argued that their influence in the day-to-day running of the NHS was very limited. This belief was associated with considerable discontent.

Health Authorities were responsible for teaching hospitals in areas with teaching hospitals and were known as AHA(T)s.

AHAs provided a point at which public interest in the NHS could be formally expressed. Facilities for collaboration between local government and the NHS at Area level were provided by Joint Consultative Committees (JCCs). In metropolitan districts there was one such committee to cover all services of common concern, and in non-metropolitan counties there were two, one covering personal social services and school health, and the other environmental health and housing. This was because in the counties the latter services were administered at district level.

Collaboration between AHAs and local government was also promoted by specialists in community medicine within the NHS, whose task was liaison with the local authorities.

Another responsibility of the AHAs was to establish and provide staff for the Family Practitioner Committees (FPCs – one in each area), although FPCs had their own statutorily delegated powers and functioned independently of the AHAs. They had thirty members, half of them appointed via the local representative committees of the various professions involved (there were eight doctors, three dentists, two pharmacists, one ophthalmic medical practioner and one optician). Of the fifteen lay members, four were appointed by the local authority and eleven by the AHA.

The RHAs had between eighteen and twenty-four members. One-third were local authority nominees, the rest direct appointees of the Secretary of State. The RHAs moderated national policies in a framework of regional objectives and strategies, within whose guidelines the AHAs could exercise their delegated powers (the use of which was subsequently monitored by the RHAs), while at the same time feeding back to the Department of Health and Social Security (DHSS) data about health needs and potential developments in their regions so contributing to the evolution of future national priorities and policies. RHAs also allocated the capital and revenue resources available to them to the various areas within their boundaries in the light of their long-term objectives and themselves provided directly certain financial and other central services (e.g. ambulances).

The RHAs were accountable to the Department of Health and Social Security, which was formed in 1968 and employed over 90,000 people at headquarters, although only 5,000 directly in the administration of the Health Service. Of the 5,000, not all were involved exclusively with the NHS; other duties included export sponsorship and supervision of the work of the Medicines Commission, as well as personal social services.

In December 1972 the health side of the DHSS was restructured in order to meet the demands of the proposed reorganization of the NHS, and it began to act as the central policy-forming, monitoring and funding body of the Health Service, as well as having other national responsibilities. The DHSS is aided by a number of advisory bodies, the most important of which is the Central Health Services Council (CHSC). There is also the Personal Social Services Council (PSSC), which plays a role similar to that of the CHSC.

There is no completely external body concerned with the formulation of specific health policies. However, a number of checks are operated by the Treasury and by Parliament through the Public Accounts Committee and the House of Commons Select Committee on Expenditure.

Emphasis after 1974 was on management by objectives. A consultative document published by the DHSS in 1971 stated:

> There is to be a fully integrated health service in which every aspect of health care is provided, so far as it is possible, locally and according to the needs of the people . . . throughout the new

administrative structure there should be clear definition and allocation of responsibilities, there should be a maximum delegation downwards, matched by accountability upwards, and a sound management structure should be created at all levels.

In fact, the 1974 reorganization was a disaster.

In the face of mounting criticism in 1976 a Royal Commission was set up to 'consider in the interests both of the patients and of those who work in the NHS the best use and management of the financial and manpower resources of the NHS'. The largely anodyne Report was published in July 1979 after a Conservative Government had taken office. From 1974 to 1982 the NHS underwent continuous evolution. It was studied incessantly; working party reports, advisory committees, too and various other reports were all published. Criticism of the 1974 restructuring were very substantial: that there were too many committees, too many administrators, too few quick decisions and that too much money was wasted was obvious to all.

In 1982 a further reorganization took place, which aimed to simplify the NHS structure in England by removing the Area tier and creating District Health Authorities instead. It sought to strengthen management at local level with greater delegation of responsibility. Then the DHSS aimed to simplify both the planning system and the professional advisory machinery. Emphasis was placed on managerial efficiency and on greater accountability of the NHS to Parliament via the Secretary of State. The Royal Commission had decided that there was one tier too many. The Area Health Authority was abolished and its powers given to the Districts, while the DHSS and the Regions remained unchanged: unaffected by 1982 reorganization, they retained their 1974 powers and positions.

The Royal Commission saw restructuring as the opportunity for introducing flexibility into NHS administration and for decentralization and simplification in terms of lines of communication and responsibility. Family Practitioner Committees now administer the contracts and services of medical practitioners, general dental practitioners, pharmacists and opticians. They deal directly with the DHSS and are centrally financed. In 1974 there was one FPC per area. In 1982 boundaries are more complex; some relate to one DHA and some to several DHAs. Despite some opposition, the Government feels that there is no justification for dissolving or replanning the independent FPC system.

In the provision of health care under the National Health Service one of the key concepts is planning. Indeed, one of the most obvious trends in most developed countries' health-care systems in recent years has been an increased tendency to assign great importance to 'comprehensive health-care planning'. According to the theorists, the planning cycle has two main elements, one strategic, the other operational. The former provides a long-term view (between ten and fifteen years) of the objectives of the services at District and Regional level as a background for the construction of shorter-term operational plans. These are established through consultation between all levels of the health service administration on a three-year rolling basis and are revised each year in relation to factors like variations in resource constraints or changes in priorities.

Once plans have been formed and agreed at all levels, their application is conducted via the system of delegated powers. Each tier monitors the performance of the one immediately below it, a process which may be compared with that of co-ordinating the planning inputs of the various individuals, advisory groups and care-planning teams at any one level, in that neither monitoring nor co-ordinating roles in themselves involve direct managerial control over those being monitored or co-ordinated.

This planning system has not gained high marks from those who are planned: doctors especially regard it as highly inefficient. There are mechanisms aimed at ensuring that NHS management is kept informed of medical and other professional opinions and that NHS policy is accepted by the professions. For example, each District has Local Professional Advisory Committees formed from some of those groups that are involved in the Community Health Services. These help to provide the basis of the statutory medical advisory machinery at both District and Regional levels. And in England above the Regional tier the Central Health Services Council and its specialist sub-committees, such as the Sub-Committee on Vaccination and Immunization, advise the DHSS on national issues. (Rather different arrangements have been made in other parts of the UK.)

The NHS is allegedly structured to give individual doctors considerable direct managerial responsibilities, as advocated by the Hunter Report (published by the DHSS in 1972). These are discharged mainly by the specialists in community medicine, the District Community Physicians (DCPs); and the Regional Medical Officers and their staffs. Their formal duties relate to the planning process, the development and evaluation of epidemiological information about their localities, the evaluation of service effectiveness, the coordination of preventive services and advice offered to local authorities.

In the Health Service public interests are deemed to be protected by the procedures available for the handling of specific grievances and by arrangements for encouraging public involvement in the development of the NHS through the Community Health Councils in England and Wales and their equivalents, the Northern Irish District Committees and the Scottish local Health Councils. Complaints are handled at a number of levels, ranging from internal verbal inquiries, which usually resolve minor hospital issues, to court cases in serious instances, such as alleged neglect or mistreatment of patients. Accusations of certain forms of misconduct against individual practitioners may be made to the appropriate professional body and in cases involving independent contractors who fail to meet their terms of service the FPCs may be called on to give judgement through the system of Service Committees established under the NHS (Service Committees and Tribunal) Regulations of 1974, a review of which was initiated by the Government in late 1976.

As a result of all this complex planning mechanism, the number of administrators grew and the planning of the National Health Service virtually seized up, so a number of further changes were made in 1982. All planning is now based on Districts, but the system still seems as ineffective as ever. Some indication of the growth of the NHS is given by the number of people it employs: about 400,000 in 1949, 713,000 in 1974 and 835,000 in 1980.

What are now seen as the major problems of running the NHS? The first is the specific problem of London. The capital has a concentration of hospitals, in an area of declining population, which gives rise to an excess of acute hospital facilities, while in contrast, primary health care is deficient. At the end of 1975 London, with a population of over 8 million, had only fifty-four health centres, whereas there were 731 in England and Wales at the end of 1977 for 50 million people. Ideally, there should be over 2,000 in the country as a whole. The second major problem is management costs: one of the criticisms of the 1974 reorganization was the greatly increased costs of administration and management. In 1980 there were over 100,000 administrative and clerical staff, a fourfold increase over those employed in 1949 compared with a threefold increase for doctors and a doubling of nurses and of all other NHS staff. The 1982 reorganization should lead to a reduction in management staff. The managerial deficiencies centre on the lack of good information. The Royal Commission said in 1979: 'Unfortunately the information available to decision makers in the NHS leaves much to be desired.' There is a lack of management innovation and development. The Health Advisory Service and development teams have now been set up. These groups visit and comment on individual hospitals and community services for the care of the mentally ill and the mentally handicapped and the long-term care of children and the elderly. A Management Advisory Service has been set up experimentally in three areas. But it is not only management that is deficient: a major criticism of the early years of the NHS was the lack of concern with prevention. More emphasis has been placed on this in recent years; the 1979 Royal Commission and the Black Report both laid great stress on prevention, as has the Social Services Committee of the House of Commons.

Stoppages and industrial action in the NHS increased considerably from 1967 to 1977, although its record was better than that of the country as a whole during the period. Some say that because health is an essential service, like the police and the firemen, NHS workers have been exploited.

Enough has been said to indicate that the NHS has several distinctive characteristics: it is free, for the most part, at the point of service; it tries to be uniform throughout; it is short on innovation; it is monolithic and bureaucratic; nowhere is it responsive to consumer demand; it is set up to handle 'patients' (those who wait); and increasingly it is run for the benefit of those who work in it.

The NHS has to cope, administratively, with a desire for a nationally uniform level of provision, while it has inherited different levels of provision – London with its teaching hospitals, for example – and innovation is inescapably uneven. Regular requests are made for the most expensive treatment, such as scanners and kidney dialysis machines, to be available on demand; the hospital administrators have to weigh up the benefits of buying such expensive equipment for a few consultants to use on a small number of patients against the benefits of equipment which is simpler and would benefit many more people. Hence there is pressure for some patients to seek treatment at expensive private hospitals with expensive equipment, which looks (and is) unfair, according to the criterion that treatment should go first to those who most urgently need it. But this criterion is not a clear one. Obviously, a major heart attack is 'urgent'; but for an elderly person with an arthritic limp every day waiting for a hip-replacement operation means one more day with contracting mobility and pain – yet hip replacement is 'cold', not urgent, surgery.

The National Health Service has an inbuilt tendency to be run on the principle that when father turns we all turn and also that we all ought to wait our turn. There is a degree of passivity in the British, as opposed to the Germans and the Americans, whose instinct is to go out and buy the treatment they need and not to wait for it. That is the philosophy of the market – that supply expands to meet demand – while an authoritarian, paternalist system such as the NHS weighs up 'urgency' by determining itself what is urgent and is always constrained by lack of public finance.

The effect of the authoritarian, paternalist system is to give power to the administrators and consultants, who allocate resources both by an appeal to what is 'just' and by means of a power struggle. The bureaucratic system is necessarily sluggish – slow to close down what has become redundant and slow to expand when demand is expanding. Demand is itself a function of the rate of innovation, since it is no use 'demanding' a course of treatment that has not yet been invented. Such a system is inherently badly adapted to a period of rapid change.

Is the NHS the only possible option for Britain? A look at Europe's different systems in chapter 10 will prove that it certainly is not.

10

The Provision of Health Care in Europe*

The United Kingdom and Italy are very much the odd men out in
Europe because in both countries a large proportion of health-care
provision falls directly on the taxpayer and because hospitals, doctors
and ambulances are provided predominantly by the state in the same
way as the police and the army are. Moreover, in each country the
service is for the most part provided free of direct charge to the patient.

In Britain, out of a total expenditure on health care of all kinds of
£13,700 million in 1981, it is estimated that only some 3 per cent was
paid for out of income and savings, partly for non-prescription
medicines. In the same year BUPA and other health insurance
agencies paid out only 1.5 per cent of total expenditure on health care,
or £205 million. A small part of the nation's health care is paid for
out of the National Insurance fund, which covers the cost of some
road accidents; otherwise since 1948 the bulk of Britain's health-care
costs have been borne by the National Health Service – some
£13,100 million in 1981, or 95.5 per cent of the total.

Elsewhere there is much more of an insurance element in the
payment for services, and the services are themselves provided by
Churches, charities, companies, trade unions, as well as by the state.
The fact that for over a third of a century the British have gone down a
different path, and have not been followed except by Italy, is
explicable in several ways. In Roman Catholic countries, like the
Republic of Ireland, the Church has been wary of direct state
involvement in medical care, as it has been of direct state involvement
in education. In many countries the medical profession has been deeply
sceptical of 'socialist' control of their work. And, historically, from

*This chapter first appeared, in a slightly different form, as a *Briefing* (Office of Health
Economics) in October 1982.

Bismarck's time on, the provision of health care has been linked to the social security system, and the idea of social insurance, with benefits on what seems to the British a lavish scale, has been a powerful tradition in Germany and the countries associated with it.

In general, a distinction may be drawn between centralized *payment* for health care and its centralized *provision*. The result of these differences of payment and provision seems to have surprisingly little effect on the outcomes, mortality and morbidity rates, or the take-up of medical care. But it has deeply affected the style of provision, the attitudes of the public and the remuneration of the doctors. Of course, some differences arise because some countries are richer than others. West Germany's wealth is reflected in its gleaming hospitals. But the differences go beyond that.

In what follows there is a brief description of the finance and the provision of health care in the countries of the European Community – including Spain but excluding Greece and Portugal, which are too poor for valid comparisons – with some numbers to indicate cost and provision. Finally, this chapter raises some questions for the organization of health care in Britain.

There are several ways of expressing the amount that is spent on health care. It can be expressed in absolute terms (so many billions of dollars or pounds), or as a percentage of the GNP (Gross National Product), or as expenditure per capita. Table 3 shows the percentage of GNP in ten European countries, including the United Kingdom.

Obviously, the richest countries spend the most, both as a proportion of GNP and per capita. That is no mystery. But several qualifications have to be advanced before simple comparisons can be made. The population at risk differs from country to country. Ireland, for example, has disproportionately more children, 31.4 per cent under 14 compared with 22 per cent in England and Wales. And that influences expenditure. Other countries have a disproportionate number of elderly people – Germany has 15.3 per cent of its population over 65, compared with 10.8 per cent in Ireland, for example. A sophisticated statistical exercise would be necessary to ensure that like was really being compared with like.

In addition, however, what is paid for a unit of service varies

Table 3   *Expenditure in health care in ten countries as a percentage of GNP, about 1980*

	% of GNP
Belgium	6.1
Denmark	6.7
France	8.1
FR Germany	8.0
Ireland	8.4
Italy	6.4
Luxembourg	9.5
Netherlands	8.7
Spain	5.4
UK	5.7

Source: OECD estimates.

Table 4   *Proportion of doctors and nursing personnel, France, FR Germany, UK, 1976*

	Doctors per 10,000 people	Nursing personnel per 10,000 people
France	16.3	57.4
FR Germany	19.9	37.1
UK	15.2	37.4

Source: Health Services in Europe, vol. 2, World Health Organization, Copenhagen, 1981.

greatly. In the United Kingdom, with a virtual monopoly supplier of health services, the price of inputs, especially the fees and salaries of doctors, nurses and paramedicals, and the costs of pharmaceuticals have been strictly controlled. In West Germany, by contrast, the relatively freer market has enabled fees to be bid up to a higher level. If (as in Table 4) facilities are compared, it can be seen that there is less disparity than might be expected from expenditure figures. Other indicators suggest different traditions in patterns of health care, resulting in a different pattern of outlays. It is not possible to say *a priori* which pattern is the 'best': the 'best' depends upon what you want.

One way of pointing out what is the 'best' is to compare outcomes – deaths, morbidity rates – though how far these outcomes are due to medical care is a debatable point. A rich country tends to have people who eat more, drink more, smoke more and travel in cars more than those in a poor one. The health services spend a great deal clearing up the consequences of affluence. Much illness also, of course, arises from poverty.

Table 5 presents some comparisons of infant mortality rates and expectation of life for men at the age of 45. It will be seen that Denmark, France and Holland have low rates of infant mortality, while Spain and Germany have high rates (though in all cases the rates are low by world standards – about 1 per cent). The expectation of life for men at 45 is again roughly the same – ranging from 26.5 years in Scotland to 29.7 in Holland. The extra three years may represent better health care, but as the Spanish figure is almost the same as the Dutch, and the Luxembourg figure is only a little better than the

Table 5   *Health indicators, Europe, 1978*

	Infant mortality per 1,000 live births	*Expectation of life, males aged 45*
Belgium	13.9	27.6 (1976)
Denmark	8.9	29.5
France	10.6	28.6 (1976)
FR Germany	14.7	28.1
Ireland	15.6 (1977)	27.7 (1975)
Italy	17.7 (1977)	28.6 (1975)
Luxembourg	9.6	27.0
Netherlands	8.1	29.7
Spain	15.1	29.5 (1976)
England and Wales	13.1	28.2 (1977)
Scotland	13.0	26.5

Source: WHO, 1981.

Scottish, it is hard to believe that the pattern or even the quality of health care makes much difference in itself.

But, of course, such gross differences are not the only (or indeed the main) indicators of health-care quality. The data illustrate the fact that the mode of payment is not of itself a direct determinant of either how much is spent or the consequent healthiness of the population.

How then, do people pay for health care? In each country two extremes may be briefly described. There is a small proportion of wealthy people, often internationally oriented, who pay for virtually all their own medical care — wealthy Arabs, for example, who patronize the fashionable practitioners in London, Monte Carlo, Paris or Zurich and who use private hospitals and clinics. There is, too, a population of grossly disabled people, mentally handicapped, seriously schizophrenic or senile, who spend their lives in publicly provided or charitable hospitals for long-stay patients. The way in which such patients are cared for is a sign of the quality of a society, but it is not necessarily an indication of the quality of medical care in general. This chapter is not about the grossly handicapped or the extremely rich, nor is it about the health care of those who serve in the armed forces or in other specialized groups. It is about the payment for health care and its provision for the great majority of the population.

It is easiest to begin at home. In the United Kingdom (and below this will usually be shorthand for England and Wales, since there are marginal differences in Scotland and Northern Ireland and it would be tedious continually to refer to them), the National Health Service has provided medical care for most people since 1948. Access to primary medical care is free. The general practitioner may be visited at his practice or at a health centre provided by the NHS, where simple procedures may be carried out, or the doctor may make domiciliary visits. Nursing and other auxiliary services are free, as are ambulances.

The general-practice doctor is paid partly on a salary, partly by a capitation fee and partly on a fee for item of service basis. There are restrictions on the number of doctors who may offer their services in any area. Pharmaceuticals are available on prescription, for which a standard charge is made of £1.30 per item. However 75 per cent of prescriptions are exempt from this charge because of patients' age, medical condition or poverty. Dental care and opticians' services are similarly available for more substantial charges. Hospital care, both in-patient and out-patient, is free, though out-patients pay the standard charge for prescriptions. The hospital staff is salaried and not paid per item of service.

The National Health Service is centrally organized but locally administered. It is financed from general taxation, with a contribution of 9 per cent from the National Insurance fund, itself financed by a compulsory pay-roll levy, and 3 per cent by patient payments.

That, then, in brief, is the British system. It is supplemented, for some 7 per cent of the population, by health insurance schemes, which provide privacy in hospitals and speedy access to medical consultation and medical and surgical treatment. Only a small minority of the 7 per cent who are so insured rely on the insurance for all their medical care.

The nearest approach to the British system – other than the Italian – is that found in Denmark. The whole population since 1973 has been covered by a compulsory health insurance scheme. There are two categories, group 1 and group 2. In group 1, covering 93 per cent of the population, there is a free choice of general practitioner, who may refer to a specialist. All medical care, inclusive of hospital care, is free. Medicines in hospital are free, and outside hospital medicines are reimbursed to the extent of 75 per cent, 50 per cent or nil. Medicines with 'valuable therapeutic effect' are reimbursed at a 50 per cent rate, and medicines used for treatment of well defined, often mortal diseases are reimbursed at 75 per cent of cost. All other medicines, including those sold over the counter are not reimbursed. For patients belonging to group 2 of the insurance scheme the general practitioner is entitled to charge the patient a sum in excess of the standard reimbursable fee. The patient can go directly to a specialist, and normally he or she has to pay him a sum in excess of the standard reimbursable fee. Pharmaceutical reimbursement is the same as in group 1. All hospital care is free.

The health service is financed by the counties, under the supervision of the National Board of Health, with part of the cost financed by the state and the rest by local (county) income tax. The reimbursement by the state takes the form of a lump-sump subsidy, the amount of which is based on objective criteria (population, age distribution, road length, etc.). This lump sump covers all medical activities in the county which can allocate the money as it so wishes.

An alternative system to a centralized tax and insurance scheme like that in Denmark is a series of insurance schemes, as in the Federal Republic of Germany. Over 90 per cent of the German people belong to a statutory health insurance scheme and a further 8 per cent to private, non-statutory insurance schemes. The statutory scheme provides virtually free health care for its members, with nominal charges for medicines, dentistry and – on a more limited scale – spectacles (every three years, except for medical reasons).

All treatment is therefore free at point of service, and the doctor or hospital is paid directly by the scheme. In the private schemes expenditure is reimbursed within set limits. The compulsory insurance schemes – over 1,400 of them – are autonomous and are divided into eight categories, whose resources are derived from compulsory levies of 7 to 14 per cent of earnings (the average is 12 per cent), divided equally between employer and employed.

Belgium has a compulsory insurance system covering virtually the whole population. There are about 1,745 sick funds providing health-care insurance, organized into six major groupings. Health-care contributions levied on employers and employees are paid, via the National Social Security Office, to the National Institute for Sickness and Invalidity Insurance, which divides them among the sick-fund groupings.

The patient pays the GP a standard fee directly and subsequently receives partial or full reimbursement from his sick fund. For a normal patient the rate of reimbursement is at present at least 75 per cent, although the Government has recently proposed that this rate of reimbursement should be reduced. Special category patients (e.g. the disabled, pensioners, widows and orphans with low incomes) receive 100 per cent reimbursement.

The doctor is free to prescribe any medicine, but there is a four-category system providing for different levels of patient contribution to the cost of the medicines prescribed. Category A (life-saving medicines) are fully reimbursed. For category B (therapeutically useful medicines, such as antibiotics) normal patients pay 25 per cent of the price up to BF 300, while special-category patients pay 15 per cent of the price up to BF 200. For category C (less useful medicines) patients pay 50 per cent of the price, with a ceiling of BF 500 for normal patients and one of BF 300 for special-category patients. Category D medicines (such as oral contraceptives) are non-reimbursable. With the first three categories the pharmacist is paid the balance of the price by the sick funds.

The patient pays the hospital a daily fee (the amount of which is regulated by law), covering nursing services, hotel costs, administration, depreciation, etc., and in addition he pays for the services of doctors and for medicines supplied. He is fully reimbursed by his sick fund in respect of the daily fee for the first forty days spent in hospital. Thereafter, if he can afford it, he has to bear part of the hotel cost element out of his own pocket. Reimbursement of the patient's payment for doctors' services and for medicines supplied is made on the same basis as for non-hospital patients.

The state pays 95 per cent of the cost of treating the social diseases (cancer, tuberculosis, poliomyelitis, mental illness and handicap).

The French health care system is financed by the social security systems (or *caisses*), which cover the whole population. They are administered by boards representative of the employers and the unions; the socialist Government's projected law will give the trade unions a majority of seats on the boards. The *caisses* impose a levy on employers and employees and, in return, finance most health care.

General practitioners are of two grades, corresponding simply to specialists and non-specialists. The 85 per cent who fall into the latter category can charge standard fees, while the rest can charge more. The social security system will refund 80 per cent of the standard charge for a consultation, subject to a maximum contribution by the assured of 100 Fr. Fr. a month, or 600 Fr. Fr. in six months. This is subject, too, to the overriding constraint that twenty-four scheduled major diseases (e.g. tuberculosis, cerebral-vascular diseases, multiple sclerosis, pernicious anaemia, etc.), or a 'twenty-fifth' that is assessed by the doctor of the social security scheme to be chronic or severe, is treated without charge. No charge is levied on those receiving 'social aid' (i.e. the poor).

Almost all hospital care is thus virtually free. The patient is required to pay 20 per cent of his hospital bill, but since hospital care runs into one or other of these barriers of expense or scheduled illness, and psychiatric and maternity beds are also provided free of charge, few charges are actually levied.

Pharmaceutical prescriptions are reimbursed on three scales: 'life-saving' medicines, or those prescribed for the twenty-four listed illnesses are free; other medicines are 70 per cent free; but a group of 'comfort medicines' – e.g. laxatives, tonics, slimming preparations – are only 40 per cent reimbursable. (Again all these charges are subject to the 100 Fr. Fr. limit of health expenditure by the patient in any one month.)

Surgical care is free if the operation is rated by a scale of gravity at or above appendicitis, known colloquially as 'K50'.

It will be seen, therefore, that the bulk of French medical care is free of charge: 99.5 per cent of hospital care in public hospitals and 66 per cent of non-hospital health care is free.

The Netherlands has a system not unlike that of France but with less comprehensive care. About two-thirds of the population is insured by a state system, which meets most of the costs of services of general practitioners, dentists, hospitals and medicines, for a levy on earnings divided equally between the employer and the employee. The rest of the population is covered by private insurance. Hospital care and specialist service is reimbursed only if referral is made by a general practitioner.

Ireland is a much poorer country than the Netherlands, but it has a relatively lavish system of health care. The population is divided into three categories. The first, the poorest, or roughly 40 per cent, assessed by a means test, receives all primary and hospital health care free, including pharmaceuticals and other treatment, as well as dentistry. A second category, some 48 per cent of the population, makes an earnings-related contribution to the health care system and in return receives free hospital and maternity care, with some reimbursement for medicines. The third category, covered by private health insurance, is about 17 per cent of the population, thus overlapping with the second category. It receives free in-patient treatment in public wards and contributions towards other fees and charges (for specialists, medicines, dentistry), but general-practitioner services must be paid, unless the insurance scheme covers that expenditure.

Luxembourg has thirty hospitals, no health centres and just over 400 physicians. Over 99 per cent of the population is covered by a sickness insurance similar to that of Denmark.

Italy is a mixture of an advanced industrial country and a rural one. Since 1979 it has had a National Health Service administered by twenty regions. The bulk of the expenditure comes from contributions paid by employers and employees through the National Provident Institute, supplemented by special taxation levied on citizens not subject to a social security scheme. This system has replaced the previous 200 or so insurance funds, whose administration ceased in December 1981.

All medical care is free of charge except for prescriptions, for which a charge is made for some medicaments. The private sector is flourishing for the better-off. There is great unevenness of provision, and the system is said to be greatly open to abuse.

Spain resembles Italy economically and socially. It has a health insurance system covering 90 per cent of the population, which reimburses all or part of the cost of medicines. The scheme is financed by the state, employers and employees on a tripartite basis, through the Instituto Nacional de Prevision. In rural areas general practitioners are paid by the state to provide free care for the insured. In towns children may be treated free by paediatricians. General practitioners in towns are reimbursed by the Instituto Nacional de Prevision. There are also free clinics for the poor, for emergencies and for persons on social security.

Health care in Europe thus presents a complex picture. Perhaps Table 6 may make it clearer. What is perhaps most surprising is that in each country most health care is either free or heavily subsidized. The differences arise in the way people pay – through taxes or by insurance

Table 6 *Health-care provision in Europe*

	Basis of Payment	GPs	'Comfort' medicines	'Serious' medicines	Specialist consultation	Hospital care	Long-term care	Dentistry
Belgium	(Ins.)	S	P	S	F	F	F	P
Denmark	(Ins.)	F	P	S	F	F	F	F
France	(Ins.)	S	P	S	S	F	F	P,F
FR Germany	(Ins.)	F	F	F	F	F	F	F
Ireland	(Tax/Ins.)	F,U	F,U	F,U	F,P	F,P	F,P	F,P
Italy	(Tax/Ins.)	F	U	S,F	F	F	F	P
Luxembourg	(Ins.)	F	F	F	F	F	F	P
Netherlands	(Ins.)	F,P	F,P	F,P	F,P	F,P	F	F,P
Spain	(Ins./Tax)	F,P,U	F,P,U	F,P,U	F,P,U	F,P,U	F	F,P,U
UK	(Tax)	F	S	S	F	F	F	P

Notes: F=free at point of service; Ins.=insurance; P=partial reimbursement; S=small charge; U=unfree.

(which usually comes to the same thing) – and whether they have to fill in forms to get their money back.

There are also geographical differences in the availability of adequate health care – paradoxically some of the poorer areas of Europe, like rural Ireland and Scotland, do best – and in its speed and 'luxury' of provision. In Britain the patient is accustomed to wait to see a hospital specialist but not in France and Germany. And in Germany (to a lesser extent in France) the hospitals are modern and have single or small rooms.

In the United Kingdom the great majority of hospitals are owned by the National Health Service (or by a parallel body in Northern Ireland) and operated on its behalf by Health Districts, with whom primary medical care teams have contracts of service. Above the Districts are the Regions, which employ the hospital consultants. It follows that the planning of provision is a central responsibility (though it is subject, for most purposes, to subordinate bodies), as are the negotiations on salaries, fees and other costs. In the United States, in direct contrast, hospitals may be operated by states and counties, by universities, by lay and religious charities, by co-operatives or by private firms. Primary-care teams are private enterprises, sometimes working as a partnership in a firm, as lawyers do. Their expenses are met by the patients, who may be reimbursed by public or private insurance.

The dichotomy between a central monopoly scheme and a spontaneous and heterogeneous health-care market is not a clear-cut one, however. The bulk of European systems fall between the two models, with Denmark and Italy being nearest the British system and Germany nearest the American. Even so, all countries make some sort of attempt at controlling costs and some effort to plan the provision of medical care.

The extremes meet in mental health. All countries provide publicly-supported hospitals for long-stay psychiatric and mental handicapped patients. No country provides intensive psychoanalysis for all patients who seek it, whether on a free-at-point-of-service basis or through insurance schemes.

In medicine and surgery most countries reimburse a high proportion of the cost of most prescribed medications and much or all of the cost of short-term hospital care. But the way in which hospitals are owned and managed varies greatly.

Historically the doctor was self employed, working alone or in partnership, and the British National Health Service recognizes that fact by paying fees and expenses generally on a per capita basis. The general practitioner is not a salaried employee. (British hospital doctors, on the other hand, are salaried employees on either a full-time or a part-time basis.) This is broadly true of all European systems, except that the doctor is usually reimbursed on a fee per item of service basis, either directly by the insurance scheme or directly by the patient, who is then reimbursed wholly or in part by the insurance scheme. In hospitals, however, the doctors are usually paid salaries. Dentists, pharmacists and opticians are almost universally paid on a fee per item of service basis.

The exceptions to this rule are to be found in the rural areas of Ireland and Spain, where the state (or the social security system) provides a dispensary, staffed by a salaried medical care team, or an individual doctor (for example, there is a salaried doctor on Clare Island, a remote community in Clew Bay off the coast of County Mayo, in Ireland). This has its origins in nineteenth-century attempts to provide basic services to remote communities, and such services, often with religious and charitable origins, are to be found in the poorer parts of many European towns, sometimes transmitted into a modern neighbourhood health centre.

In Britain the medical profession has been more or less divided into two, the general practitioners and the hospital doctors who provide specialist treatment. Sometimes the general practitioner runs a clinic in a hospital, and specialists occasionally make domiciliary visits, but generally the roles are in practise distinct. In continental Europe this division is less apparent. Patients will turn directly to different doctors for different problems. Some health insurance systems require a referral by a general practitioner (as a means of limiting expenditure, since specialist consultations are more expensive). Nevertheless, quite small towns will have streets with rows of brass plates modestly advertising specialists in skin diseases, obstetrics, gynaecology, chest and thoracic problems, allergies or psychiatry, to which the local population will turn directly. In Germany, for example, over half the 56,000 specialist physicians practise outside hospitals.

These doctors often have beds in the local hospitals, as was once almost universally the case in Britain and still is in rural areas with small 'cottage' hospitals. In France a specialist is allowed two 'private' beds for every forty within the public sector. The hospitals themselves are provided by a variety of means. In Britain they are owned by the state. In Denmark they are owned by the counties. They are publicly owned by eight regional health boards in Ireland, although there are voluntary hospitals, sometimes provided by religious orders, whose costs are reimbursed mainly by the insurance scheme. For the most part these voluntary hospitals are university teaching hospitals. In Belgium the hospitals are provided by public social aid centres (formerly the Poor Law authorities) and by mutual aid societies and religious bodies. In France the hospitals are provided by communes, by religious orders or by private bodies, all supervised by Regional Directorates of Hospitals and the Inspectorate-General of Health to make sure that the number and type of beds provided is appropriate to the demand. The current costs of the public hospitals are met by reimbursement from the social security system. In Germany about half the hospital beds are in hospitals owned by the *Länder* or town councils; one-third are run by charities; and the remainder are privately operated. In Italy the hospitals are publicly funded by the National Health Service but administered by autonomous boards representing the local political parties.

Curiously enough, only in the United Kingdom and Denmark are ambulances regarded as a social service. In Belgium, for example, ambulance services are provided by the Red Cross and by private organizations. In France there is an agreed scale of charges, met by the social security system, for ambulances provided by the Red Cross or private firms.

Each country also has a publicly provided system of community health care, health education, medical research, control of pharmaceuticals, sanitary inspection, public health laboratories and occupational and school health-care provision. The same problems affect all health-care provision and development, whatever the structure of finance and control.

Are there any general lessons to be derived from this review of Europe's health-care provision?

First, the control of costs. In state-provided sectors the main means of cost control is by negotiation with the professions over salaries and fees and the cost of pharmaceuticals and other supplies. This puts a limit on costs and hospital budgets, so that in effect the supply of medical care is rationed, chiefly by allowing waiting lists for consultation and treatment to grow or diminish. In the insurance systems such mechanisms are more difficult to operate. The doctor often decides on his own fee. The insurance scheme can set the maximum it will reimburse, leaving the patient to negotiate the remainder. (The doctor may charge, say, £50; the set insurance fee may be £40, of which 75 per cent is reimbursed. The patient thus pays the doctor £20). The effect of this escalation of costs is to make insurance schemes less viable.

Second, the viability of insurance. As costs have escalated, so contributions have increased. Few public schemes are funded; they are based (like the National Insurance scheme or the French social security system) on a pay-as-you-go principle. Resistance to increased contributions, which are in effect a form of income tax, has driven more and more schemes to seek state assistance from general tax funds. Thus in Denmark and Ireland the contribution made directly from tax has to a great degree superseded the insurance basis.

Third, exclusions. In all systems there is special provision for the indigent and for long-term sick or mentally handicapped patients. These have sooner or later to be integrated into the rest of the health-care system.

Fourth, planning of provision. General practitioners usually 'set up shop' and act as entrepreneurs. Poorer and remote areas need special treatment if adequate provision is to be made. For that reason salaried services are common in rural Ireland. Increasingly, too, the concept of the primary health-care team has developed, requiring a fully staffed and equipped health centre. This concept is furthest advanced in Britain and Denmark. It is contrary, however, to the tradition of direct access to the specialist in continental Europe.

Specialists in Britain and Denmark practise for the most part in hospitals. Local doctors' access to hospitals is more common in other countries. One consequence that was detected by the European Collaborative Hospital Study* is that in Limerick and Londonderry more consultations and investigations take place in hospital than in Colchester, where only the seriously ill are admitted to hospital. In Britain the Resource Allocation Working Party principles have been applied since 1975 to bring about a better geographical distribution of resources.

The pattern of hospital provision is a reflection of history. In countries like Germany adaptation takes place as a result both of pressure by patients through the insurance system, as they demand extra care, and of local authorities, mutual funds, charities and private bodies responding to that pressure or anticipating it. For example, German insurance schemes pay for treatment at spas. In spas all over Germany there has been a substantial growth of therapeutic and hotel provision to meet the demand. In Britain, in contrast, medical opinion is against spa treatment, and the hospitals at Droitwich, Bath and elsewhere have either closed or given it up. In Britain hospital provision is altered as a result of 'expert' opinion (modified by public pressure) about which specialities should grow and which should decline. To take one treatment as an example, cardiac surgery meets only two-thirds of the internationally recommended quantity and is one-fifth as common as in the United States, where provision is demand-led.

In France the two-approaches are reconciled by a planning process under the Commissariat au Plan, which seeks to raise supply to meet demand by stimulating investment in both the public and private sectors, but makes little or no contribution to the withdrawal of redundant facilities.

Fifth, geographical imbalance. In Alan Maynard's and Anne Ludbrook's essay 'Thirty Years of Fruitless Endeavour?' (1981) an attempt is made, on the basis of the 1977 data, to illustrate regional differences in France, the Netherlands and England. In England the

*London School of Hygiene and Tropical Medicine, 1980.

co-efficient of variation for doctors was 0.092, while in France it was 0.257 and in the Netherlands 0.282. For hospital beds in England it was 0.109, in France 0.179 and in the Netherlands 0.153. Thus in France and the Netherlands the best provided region had two and a half times more doctors per head than the worst provided, and in England less than two-fifths more. The English had 50 per cent more beds in the best provided region, while in France the figure was double and in the Netherlands nearly double. If the objective of health-care policy is in some sense to equalize geographical provision, then it is clear that the National Health Service has more powerful means of doing so than the other systems.

Sixth, social imbalance. Maynard and Ludbrook conclude that the lowering of financial barriers to health-care consumption has not been particularly successful in achieving greater social equality, a conclusion endorsed by the Black Report. It seems that on crude measures of outcome (e.g. mortality) and of input (expenditure, doctors, etc.) significant inequality continues to exist and may even have increased over the last twenty years. This dictum applies to Britain and France, but it is widely accepted that it is more generally applicable. It follows therefore that neither the mode of finance nor the form of provision of health care has made much difference to equality of access to health care.

This brief survey of European health care ends with a set of questions. It seems fairly clear that despite the difference between centralized tax-based funding of health care and insurance-based funding, the differences in how one pays, as perceived by the patients, are small. Throughout Europe most care is free when you are ill. Is it true to say, therefore, that it does not much matter whether the United Kingdom shifts to an insurance-based scheme or not? Do people on the Continent think they are getting what they pay for because they have insurance? Or do the British think that a 'free' service is a social right which they value greatly? Is there anything to be said for the fact that insurance systems seem to give administrative roles to trades unionists and businessmen (as in the former British Friendly Societies) and that their involvement is desirable on general grounds?

More profoundly, there is a major distinction between modes of *payment* and modes of *provision*. William Beveridge wrote in *Full Employment in a Free Society* (1944): 'Removal of economic barriers between the patient and treatment is only a minor step, even for cure of disease. The real task lies in the organization of the health service.' It has been assumed in the United Kingdom that because most health care is centrally funded, it has to be centrally provided. This is not axiomatic. It would be possible, for example, for all hospitals to be 'private', in the sense that they invoiced the NHS for each item of service and cut their coats according to their cloth. Perhaps the most striking effect of a visit to the Continent by somebody from the United Kingdom is awareness of the diversity of methods of provision of care there, compared with its relative uniformity here. Is there a way of reconciling centralized finance and overall planning with greater diversity of provision? It is upon this question, perhaps, that those who contemplate any long-term restructuring of the National Health Service might dwell.

11

The Future

A health service can be run in two different ways. One way is for the state to provide and for services to be made available to all and sundry. Inescapably, such a system is wasteful, in the sense that it under-provides for some people and over-provides for others, and a complex bureaucracy is necessary to organize and police it. But it is popular because when people are in desperate need and desperately frightened, it brings help and reassurance – and it is 'free', outside the cash nexus. As we have seen, however, it offers less choice and less satisfaction than services elsewhere. But almost all the evidence of opinion polls and political parties' attitudes to reforms suggest that the main structure of a state-provided national health service, freely available to all at point of use, is widely approved of in the United Kingdom.

The second way to run a health service is for those providing medical care to sell it – general-practitioner services, drugs, appliances, hospital care – like any other set of commodities and services, and for people to buy as they think fit. This is, of course, a description of health care for the rich in all countries, and they seem to find it satisfactory. In principle, as with any other service, supply and demand should balance, and steady progress should take place in the level of provision and quality of the product. But in practice most health care of this kind is covered by insurance, buttressed by a base of free state provision for the poor chronically ill who cannot pay for their own care. The reason for insurance is simple. It is to spread over relatively prosperous years the payment for a major illness.

These two extremes indicate that there is a spectrum of health-care provision. In no country is all medical care provided completely free by the state, and in no country is all medical care bought and sold. The question is: in what direction should the trend of payment and provision go – towards more state control and finance or less? It will already be clear from this book that the issues are complex, for the simple reason that 'health care' is a term that embraces a whole range of facilities and demands. Let us, then, try to clear the ground.

The World Health Organization's aim of perfect health for everybody can never be attained. This statement is not as banal as it might seem, since it was once thought – and the idea still may remain at the back of everybody's mind – that one determined push to do away with ill-health will leave relatively little for doctors and others to do. That is as unrealistic as thinking that cleaning one's teeth once a year will be enough for oral hygiene. The body and mind are complex; things, big and little, go wrong all the time and need putting right. Much that goes wrong puts itself right, of course, but a lot does not.

So even medical progress will not reduce the need for medical care. On the other hand, smallpox and measles and a host of other diseases have effectively disappeared, especially in the richer countries, and some other illnesses will follow suit. But as more and more conditions become treatable, so the demand for treatment will rise. At the moment somebody with schizophrenia can be looked after with difficulty. Some patients may soon be able to be treated effectively and probably cured – that is, there will be a demand for treatment. The initial costs of successfully treating the first few patients may be very high; as experience is gained and technology advances, the costs per case will drop, but as more and more cases are treated the total costs of what will by then be a successful treatment will rise. The total impact on expenditure will be a race between progress in treatment and the number of cases that can be treated. It is likely that the net balance will be more expenditure rather than less, though in the distant future the prospects are too uncertain for accurate forecasts to be made.

At present it does not seem likely that people will live longer, though the age of female death is still creeping up. What does seem highly likely is that as people grow older they will be less disabled and will suffer less – whether that can be called 'happiness' is a philosophical question. All the evidence suggests that people will be prepared to pay for this outcome. The main issue is whether they will want to pay directly, by insurance or by taxation. I shall argue that it will be by all these modes.

Consider the lifecycle of a family. When contraception first came in, men bought sheaths. With the coming of the Pill, contraception became a medical matter. Prescription and provision is now, for the most part, state-aided or free to the client. There will be considerable progress in contraception by means of the long-term Pill. It is in the interests of the public as well as of individuals to make 'every child a wanted child', as the Family Planning Association slogan has it. I conclude, therefore, that the greater part of family planning will be publicly provided.

Abortion, I would judge, will decline from its present level of 130,000 cases a year as a direct result of improved contraception techniques. There is no question that contraceptives can be provided perfectly satisfactorily under existing arrangements, which imply a degree of medical supervision for only a few techniques, notably the Pill, but abortion must remain entirely a matter for the medical and social services. Roman Catholics disapprove of both procedures, though the majority of Roman Catholics in fact use contraception; the rest of the population not only supports contraception and accepts abortion, but regards them as facilities that should be provided by the state, or purchased, virtually at will.

Once childbirth is under way there is, again, a strong public interest in providing the best antenatal, obstetric and postnatal care for every mother. Obviously, many families will choose to pay for this themselves, but there is already a structure of care in the NHS, which used to be of relatively poor calibre but has improved in recent years. It would seem only prudent, especially with the present low birth rate, to universalize this service and constantly to improve it. (There is, for instance, a great need for more single rooms in maternity hospitals; for some reason hospital planners have had a positive mania for communal living, perhaps representing the unthinking and brutalist 'lefty' position of so many prominent architects, or perhaps a legacy from the Poor Law tradition of work houses/infirmaries.) The regular series of checks on pregnant women and on newly-born babies and infants, accompanied in the latter case by immunization and health education, has led to a fall in neo-natal mortality, the early identification of handicaps such as deafness and the reduction of severe childhood illness.

The care of children of school age or, indeed, from toddler age onwards is inseparable from the question of family care, that is, the future of the health-care team. There has been a major report on child health, the Court Report, much of which has not been implemented. Whether its proposals are right or wrong, its thorough examination of the question is unlikely to be bettered, especially when its findings are put alongside those of the Warnock Report on special education, most of which is now on the statute book and in force.

A central fact which needs to be grasped firmly is that the care of the child as a whole cannot be left to a series of specialists who never communicate with each other or with parents, teachers, social workers, doctors or nurses. They are *all* responsible for the child's progress, and the cross-checking of data and opinions on each child is an essential part of the monitoring service that is necessary if symptoms are to be spotted early. Apart from cruelly disabling handicaps, children now suffer from three kinds of medical problem: minor illnesses (coughs, colds and the like); mild handicap, such as low IQs and mild deafness; and psycho-social disorders, which may perhaps manifest themselves as behavioural problems or under-achievement and whose origins lie in stress. Leaving aside the minor illnesses, which we all have to weather and for which medical intervention is barely necessary, the other two matters are not necessarily medical problems at all. Above all, they require handling, monitoring and steady support, both at home and at school. Although the basic diagnosis of mild handicaps and psycho-social disorders is a joint matter for doctors and other professionals, the treatment or management of the problem or difficulty will be largely a non-medical process.

Because in the future so many patients will present problems that are social as well as medical, the primary health-care team will increasingly replace the general practitioner, inescapably in the case of children. The recommendation of the Court Report, therefore, that in a group of doctors one should specialize in paediatrics, was well meant, but it is at variance not only with the idea of a 'family doctor' but also with the actual nature of the problems that face families with children and adolescents.

While many families will wish in all these respects to make their own arrangements for medical care and for education, and will feel the need to call on resources other than their own privately financed network only at moments of crisis (such as a serious physical accident, or serious social problem like drug addiction, or delinquency), many other families will not only be content with but will actively demand a publicly provided system of medical care.

The lifecycle of a family moves on to the point at which the couple's children have grown up. This is the group which is most seriously attacked by heart disease (especially the men), cancer and the psychiatric and social problems discussed in chapter 4. Then, as age comes on, the problems discussed in chapter 5 arrive.

The need for consultations about health declines from childhood to middle age, then it begins to rise, and as people reach their sixties, rises rapidly. The need for acute and long-term hospital care arises principally from the major killers and from osteo-arthritis, rheumatism and the growing difficulties of old age. The care that is necessary for the middle-aged and the 'early elderly' can be provided on demand, and there is no reason why most people should not pay for it as the need arises, provided that they are insured against the most severe problems needing surgery or intensive medical care.

It is easy to see that a fee per item of service would actively discourage the habit of regular consultation and check-up which is at the heart of adequate preventive care, particularly for children and young people and especially in the delicate area of psycho-social problems. It would be better if both medical and social help could be paid for together in some way.

Three further considerations present themselves: first, it is impossible to divorce the care of children from the care of a whole family. It would be bad medicine to do so. It follows, then, that the care of children will be, in essence, part of the arrangements made for the care of families. It is also essential to see that, wherever possible, the elderly are regarded as part of the family. Like the rest of the population, they need information and advice and the latest diagnostic tools, if only because their pattern of illness differs from that of other age groups.

Secondly, it would be helpful if all relevant information on the

127

individual and his family was capable of being assembled rapidly and digested speedily. This is obviously essential, for example, when illness is genetic in origin or in the case of infectious outbreaks like food poisoning, but it is critical, too, for efficient monitoring both of the handicapped, who (broadly defined, as in the Warnock Committee's Report) certainly comprise several millions of the population, and of the side-effects of drugs. A central part of modern medical practice therefore, is not only adequate record-keeping but also access to records kept by others, notably the hospital, the school and the social services. In recent years the process of record-keeping has been revolutionized. Whatever the legal and moral implications may be, it is not only desirable but essential that all relevant information be available to the medical practitioner, whether he be in private practice or a public servant. In the context of the virtually immediate availability of information today, no professional should have to struggle alone, without an information network, to provide adequate medical care. This is perhaps a controversial idea because it raises suspicions, legitimate problems, about confidentiality and apparent threats to independent judgement.

The third consideration is no less a threat to independence. It is the primary care team's access to advanced diagnostic facilities, and, to a lesser extent, the ability to use complex techniques of treatment. The doctor's stethoscope has been largely superseded by routine analysis of blood and urine, minor X-rays and many other tests, and his treatment can include minor surgery and physiotherapy, as well as the prescription of drugs and the offer of advice and counselling.

In short, the local primary health-care team requires, if it is to provide its patients with an adequate service, the equivalent of a fully equipped health centre and perhaps short-stay beds, especially in rural areas. The virtual universalization of what is at present patchy provision is strongly to be recommended.

The question of how this is to be organized is linked closely with the provision of hospital services and of preventive medicine, but a glance at the reasons why patients at present consult general practitioners (see chapter 2) and a study of the complex administration of the National Health Service (see chapter 9) lead to two possible conclusions.

The Future

Whether or not local health centres are financed from general taxation (as the NHS is at present) or by insurance (as in most of continental Europe and the United States), any attempt to charge the patient generally by item of service would probably prove destructive of much of the better side of medical and social care. On the other hand, there is no reason why the practitioners should not be remunerated on that basis, as pharmacists, dentists and opticians are, instead of (broadly) on a per capita basis. If, as is to be expected, more medical care is put into the hands of the primary health-care team, then expenditure on it will rise. This implies larger budgets.

The merit of paying for the service by a mixture of payments per item and per capita is that a formula can be devised which leaves each health centre virtually autonomous, with a minimum of bureaucratic structure above it. It is, therefore, highly desirable that what is now a group practice of, say, six doctors, caring between them for about 15,000 patients, should become a practical and autonomous basis for health care in a community. A health centre on this scale would be a substantial enterprise, employing more than twenty-five people – paramedicals, a pharmacist, secretaries – and requiring close communication with all other medical and social institutions in the locality. It is hard to imagine that its budget would be less than £500,000 a year (at 1983 prices). There is no administrative reason why patients should not top up any state scheme of finance with contributions of private fees, plus whatever private insurance might provide.

What would be the point of paying extra? In general practice, this problem scarcely arises outside central London where the rich, both British and foreign, pay for the teaching hospitals' consultants and where the major private hospitals are situated. It does in dentistry because it is widely thought that the level of expertise and, above all, the time taken over treatment, is greater in the private than in the public sector.

It is evident that the massive increase in health care expenditure now envisaged could not be financed wholly from public funds without causing serious problems for the Exchequer. The time has come for a realistic discussion of what people might pay for. Half the total of prescriptions now attract a substantial fee. A charge for a consultation at a health centre or a hospital could well become one of the normal expectations of patients, provided that certain people were exempted on the grounds that their incomes were low (we have seen that such a category would not include by any means all families with children or elderly people) and provided also that treatment associated with 'catastrophic' events – notably the major killers – was paid for either by the state or by insurance.

The only way to channel extra resources into the health-care system is to cut down unnecessary expenditure by charging those able to pay for routine care and by encouraging people to take out insurance against the costs of treatment for major illness. Over 2 million people are covered by BUPA and other insurance schemes, and the possibility of expansion is real, but such an expansion will not occur until people realize that modern medicine is expensive and has to be paid for.

The field to which this issue of individual payment by the client for services rendered is most relevant is, paradoxically, preventive medicine. People are used to paying a great deal for sport and recreation. They are used (to a lesser extent) to paying for counselling through organizations like Weight Watchers. They are used to paying for the routine testing of much of their stock of consumer durables – cars, central heating and so on. There seems no reason, in principle, why more and more aspects of preventive medicine should not be paid for by the clients, or why contributions should not be made by local authorities. The biggest area of expansion in primary health care will be the drive for positive health through exercise, recreation and counselling on relaxation and reduction in tension. This is still a grossly underfunded area of national life although it is one to which much private expenditure is already directed.

A major programme of positive health implies, then, the linking of medical facilities to sport and leisure facilities, not necessarily physically, of course, but conceived as a whole, embraced (as it were) intellectually as part of the same process of improving health. It is by no means obvious that leisure facilities should be provided publicly – golf courses on the whole are not, swimming pools on the whole are; across the whole range of active leisure it might be best if the role of public money were to offer selective support rather than actively to manage the various facilities that are desirable. In this context the more that responsibility for local health amenities is left in local hands, the more likely they are to be efficiently managed – and this broadens the scope of what it has become fashionable to call 'privatization' but is perhaps better thought of as the process of hiring competitive contractors rather than using direct local authority management and labour to provide facilities. But to suggest this is to imply, of course, that there should be diversity both in the nature of provision and in its standards. Since much of the administrative burden of the NHS is designed to achieve uniformity, this needs to be changed.

It has already been seen that uniformity is not compatible with medical progress, since new techniques are developed at a few centres and then spread to the system as a whole. Nor, at present, is treatment equally distributed. The better-off get better health care, just as all the evidence shows that, on average, their children get the best out of the school and university system. If deliberate attempts were made to *worsen* services for them, in order to spend more on the poor, the inevitable consequence would be the growth of private medicine, just as the public schools have flourished because of the inadequacies of much local authority secondary education. What is needed is not uniformity but diversity. As long as everybody has access to adequate primary medical care and to hospital care for major problems, there is no merit in providing exactly the same level of medical treatment for all, any more than there is in supplying people with identical houses or clothes. The passion for uniformity arises from a misplaced notion that medical care is 'urgent' and 'essential'. Some of it is: most of it is not.

An area of positive health that particularly needs attention is that of safety, at home, at work and on the roads. Here substantial steps have already been taken, but even now it is not fully appreciated in many quarters how frequently accidents occur or how many would be preventable by sound design and careful thought. The allocation of more resources to accident prevention – for example, for seat belts and better engineered roads – would be a substitute for providing facilities for the treatment of accidents. Even more to the point, perhaps, is the urgent necessity to eliminate smoking and to reduce excessive drinking.

No substitute has been found for the price mechanism, and it is a scandal that cigarettes (especially) during the 1970s became relatively cheaper and (to a lesser extent) alcohol as well. It is not necessary to advocate a puritan society; we should seek merely to advocate two steps – the raising of taxes on smoking, which would reduce substantially the incidence of cancer and heart disease, and the raising of the prices of alcohol, which would reduce substantially the level of alcoholism in our society.

Nevertheless, having said that the programme advocated here is not puritanical (in the pejorative sense), it must be conceded at once that it does consist of an attempt to make society change its way of life and to adopt a regimen that would be regarded by many as distinctly puritanical. Pills and potions cannot cure a lifestyle that itself causes illness.

Accordingly, the priority for public action is to tax (or even forbid) as many harmful activities as possible, especially tobacco, alcohol and the causes of accidents. Government should subsidize active leisure and recreation – how best this subsidy should be paid and allocated is a matter for detailed discussion elsewhere – and we can hope that in addition to the direct subsidy of medical services (for tax or insurance), topped up by private payments, the local health centre will become a focus of community medical care in a positive as well as a more conventional manner.

This conception of the primary health-care system clearly affects the two major groups of the community whom it has been agreed should be mainly cared for at home – the elderly, and the mentally ill. In principle, special services for these groups should be linked to the primary health-care team.

That brings us to the main issue: the future of the hospital service. It is seen now, and has for many years been seen, as the central feature of the National Health Service for a perfectly understandable set of reasons: it deals with birth and death and with serious illness; it is where the most able specialists work; it is at the forefront of medicine; and it is the system by which all doctors and nurses are trained. It is hardly surprising, therefore, if the average voter takes for granted the arrangements for providing the local doctor but thinks that the preservation – indeed, the enlargement – of the hospital service is the be-all and end-all of adequate medical care. It has been argued that more and more routine diagnostic testing and routine care has been drifting to the hospital and that a determined effort should be made to undertake this work locally. Indeed, there may well be a case for differentiating between local hospitals, which have some of the characteristics of the local health centre, and the more advanced diagnostic and treatment centres. Any organization of the hospital system, therefore, should be so designed that it encourages the local health centres to undertake as much routine care as possible.

The same doctrine applies to the elderly, the chronically sick, the severely handicapped, especially those with severe mental illness or mental handicap. It has already been argued that medical and social progress has reduced the need for the institutionalization of many of these patients, and it is virtually certain that progress will accelerate. It follows, therefore, that a decreasing proportion of the hospital service will be devoted to institutional care of this kind, though what institutional care remains will have to be of a higher standard than now generally prevails. Leaving this matter of long-term care on one side for the moment, then, the question to be addressed concerns the size of acute hospital provision, its organization and its finance.

Here, again, two contrary tendencies are at work. As new medical techniques become available, the cost of treatment per case is likely to rise initially and then to fall. The number of treatable cases will also increase in several major fields, notably cancer and heart disease. Much of the subsequent treatment will be 'routinized' and so leave the hospital for the health centre, while the length of stay per case will probably continue to fall. The net effect of this series of changes is likely to be a reduction in the number of beds, a rise in the number of in-patients, a fall in the number of out-patients and a rise in the cost per case as more 'high technology' medicine is brought to bear.

It will be essential to develop closer communications between hospitals and local health teams. This has been one of the stated objectives of the National Health Service reforms, but it has been a notable failure. The development of modern communications technology, however, should make such communication far simpler. For example, computerized hospital records ought to be mutually compatible with general practice records, which in turn should be linked to pharmacies and other paramedical specialities. The problems of confidentiality are obvious but no greater, in principle, than the present cumbrous piles of paper that form patients' records; and the advantages of instantaneous access by doctors and their teams to full medical data are self-evident. It is therefore essential that whatever else happens, over the next ten years a serious effort must be made to bring data-processing and record-keeping up to date. This will represent a breakthrough not only in patient care – since everybody ought to know more fully what everybody else is doing for a patient – but also in diminishing bureaucracy.

Hospital health-care costs have risen both because of more expensive treatment and because of the explosion of numbers in the administrative tail and the army of relatively low paid and very unproductive ancillary workers. The cause of this has been administrative breakdown. The best solution to administrative breakdown is to abolish administration and then start again. If you ask the question 'What is it for?', most administration problems solve themselves. The complex administration of the National Health Service serves – or purports to serve – three fundamental purposes.

(1) Communication and shared decision-making at the relatively local level and, to a far lesser extent, at the regional, national or international level. As has been suggested, much of this communication can now easily be coped with by adequate technological investment. The so-called 'co-ordination' brought about by endless committees is illusory.

(2) Control of costs and staffing levels. This has manifestly not been brought about by the present system. A new system is proposed below.

(3) An attempt to equalize the facilities and cost of National Health Service provision from region to region and from district to district. As chapter 10 shows, this has been more successful in Britain than elsewhere but chiefly (one suspects) by levelling down rather than by levelling up.

In short, a huge administrative superstructure exists predominantly to control costs and allocate resources. By far the simplest way to do this is for the funding agency to pay a unit per item of service. Thus if a hospital were taken as the unit, then its income could be x appendectomies, y normal births and so on, until the payments (retrospectively) covered the costs. This is the French and German system, and it requires a standard cost per unit of treatment (with a fall-back for exceptional cases). To this teaching hospitals could add grants for research, with their university income calculated in the usual way.

This would require every hospital and each department within the hospital to have a budget. This is not a departure from current practice. What would be a departure would be for each item of service to be invoiced. This raises the question of who would pay the invoice.

It is impossible to have two systems of payment, one for local health care and another for hospitals, since (for example) to make one free and to charge for the other would be to bias demand in the direction of the free service. It follows, therefore, that local health care should also invoice per item of service. It has been shown, however, that for major parts of local health care to be effective it is essential that it should be free at point of service, as is the case at present in all European countries.

There are equally strong arguments for the hospital service to be treated similarly. This suggests, therefore, a central fund, or a series of regional funds, from which the bulk of health care costs would be reimbursed. It has already been shown that it is of little importance whether the fund is called 'insurance' or 'taxation'. But it is essential that each budgetary unit in the system should be autonomous and should have an incentive to economize as much as possible in its administration.

If payment were per unit of service, it would be perfectly possible to include private payment in the system, since if £x were allowed for a hip operation, for example, then 10 per cent could be added for a private room and 30 per cent for immediacy. Moreover, there is no reason why the standard cost per item should not be paid to private hospitals and clinics; in fact, if every hospital and clinic were autonomous, the distinction would virtually disappear.

But that leaves two questions. The first is: who is to provide the capital for new investment? It must be accepted that the number of hospitals and of hospital beds is certain to continue to diminish. So what is at issue is expansion for new specialities and areas of population growth. If each major county were allocated £*x* million for capital expenditure based on the number of patients, regardless of whether its population were declining or not, then the expansion – the greater part – could be raised by charity or private investment or voted by Parliament. For example, Greater London, which is an area with a declining population, might receive, say, £100 million every year, plus so much for extra specialities, so much for research and so much raised privately; the point is that all of this would be allocated to, or raised by, units which would be wholly accountable for the use they made of it to themselves and their patients and staff. What was saved on current expenditure could be used for capital expenditure but not the other way round.

The importance of looking at things from this point of view is that there would be tremendous pressure to cut unnecessary costs. Immediately, of course, the outcry would be that it was 'unfair'. The less successful units would be those dealing with the poor. But this would not be so. If a standard payment per unit of treatment were agreed, then there is every reason to think that resources would flow to those areas that are at present judged to be under-funded. But all would depend, of course, upon the setting of the price per unit.

This would have to be agreed nationally. It has been the cause of cost escalation in insurance schemes in Germany and the USA, though it is not inevitable that this should be so an average of 'observed' costs, with a built-in drive towards economy, should be the norm. Moreover, the necessity to spend money on the basis that if a surplus were yielded, it would be available for expansion would itself be a powerful incentive to economize. It is a scandal, for example, that in Britain only 0.2 per cent of hospital cleaning and catering costs are now contracted out. The proportion should be well over half.

It would be essential, too, to challenge the idea of national scales of wages and salaries. If there were, say, some 2,000 units of health care – hospitals and health centres – negotiating according to individual and local circumstances, some wages, salaries and fees might rise and others might fall, but in every case the emphasis would be upon higher productivity, better pay and fewer people in non-essential roles.

The crux of the proposal, therefore, is that each hospital or health-care team should be in essence autonomous (though linked with others by modern technology for information about patients), with standard payments per unit of service. The sources of standard payments might be diverse – the state, insurance or private contributions; provided that the basic income of a unit was guaranteed, it could survive.

This raises the next important question, which is that of planning. How would resources be allocated? There would be two objectives. The first would be to set up the desired level of public expenditure on health care. What individuals spent in excess of this – whether directly, or indirectly through insurance – would be their affair. It follows, therefore, provision would expand as private expenditure required – as it has in recent years in the case of private hospitals and nursing homes – or as public policy decides. Here it would be essential to set public expenditure norms, per item or per person, rather than to decide centrally what facilities should be opened or closed, because if a unit were able to render services to patients or to the community, that would itself guarantee its survival and growth; if it could not render such services, it would close. The second objective would be to ensure that what was allocated was spent effectively. *That* should be the basis of health-care planning: to provide services that people actually need and want. On the environmental and preventive side provision should be the product of central allocation (for example, of resources for immunization) and attracting a clientele (for example, for physical recreation).

This policy conclusion, that supply should follow demand, is an important one. The eradication of inequality, so eagerly sought by the Merrison Report on the National Health Service and by the so-called Black Report, largely inspired by Professor Peter Townsend, a social administrator and adviser to the Labour Party, is not the best policy. What is needed is the creation of adequate norms. Beyond that it is essential to allow people to promote their own health actively.

The Future

The emphasis of this book has been upon change – and on the need to take into account, when thinking of the future, the fact that some diseases will become less virulent and others may disappear, to recognize the diminishing role of hospitals in routine care and the increasing value of the primary health-care team, to understand the growth of preventive medicine and positive health care and to realize that if there is the possibility that an illness or a handicap may be alleviated, then people will demand that help. Medical care will shift from life-saving to life-enhancement.

The cost of all this growth will extend beyond the scope of public funds; people will have to pay directly, by insurance and by taxation. I have argued that capital for expansion should be raised privately as well as being provided by the state and should be allocated according to demand, and that escalating costs should be controlled by tighter budgeting, by more autonomy within the health service, by direct and standard payment to hospitals and health centres for each unit of service and by greater flexibility. I have argued further that the process of change is such that much of the debate about the future of health care has become sterile and out of date. In planning for the next thirty years it is vital to think of the problems that will arise in the future and to propose solutions to them.

Index